SAY THE THING

Boundary-Setting Scripts &
Phrases to Communicate Directly
& Speak Up with Kindness

SAY THE
THING

KAMI ORANGE
BOUNDARY COACH

HAY
HOUSE

HAY HOUSE, INC.
Carlsbad, California • New York City
London • Sydney • New Delhi

Published in the United States by: Hay House, Inc.: www.hayhouse
.com® • **Published in Australia by:** Hay House Australia Pty. Ltd.: www
.hayhouse.com.au • **Published in the United Kingdom by:** Hay House
UK, Ltd.: www.hayhouse.co.uk • **Published in India by:** Hay House Publishers India: www.hayhouse.co.in

Project editor: Ashten Evans
Cover design: Jordan Wannemacher
Interior and cover layout: Bryn Starr Best
Interior photo of Kami: Alisha Shaw Photography

Cataloging-in-Publication Data is on file at the Library of Congress

Tradepaper ISBN: 978-1-4019-7612-5
E-book ISBN: 978-1-4019-7613-2
Audiobook ISBN: 978-1-4019-7614-9

10 9 8 7 6 5 4 3 2 1
1st edition, February 2024

Printed in the United States of America

This product uses papers sourced from responsibly managed forests.
For more information, see www.hayhouse.com.

Lora Nyx,
This book exists because you went first.
Haaayyy??

Contents

A Journey to
Saying the Thing

The purpose of this book is to teach you how to say the thing. What does it mean to say the thing?

Saying the thing means setting boundaries, speaking up in defense of others, and confidently asking for what you want.

My hope is this book will guide you to develop the personal habit of saying the thing, and together we'll create more kind and direct communication in the world.

First, we'll cover the four choices we have when setting boundaries, define what a boundary is, and talk about why we struggle with them. Next are three build-your-own boundary scripts to know what to say in both public and private. Finally is the largest section of the book: hundreds of kind, direct, and bold phrases to give you ideas of how to respond on any popular topic.

I've collected boundary phrases for years, and this book includes my favorites as well as custom responses I wrote for my students and clients. I hope after reading this book, your boundary-setting journey will not be as long and winding as the one I had to take.

My journey began with a strange childhood. I was raised by religious extremists in Utah, in the United States. We had daily conversations about repentance and the end of times. We covered our bodies in loose-fitting clothing to be "modest." Most popular books, movies, and music were considered too sexual or violent, including the Josh Groban CD I was given by a classmate and which my parents immediately snapped in half due to the "explicit lyrics." There were rules about what jokes we could laugh at, what words we could use, and what thoughts were appropriate to think. We ate only raw fruits and vegetables, leading to my siblings and me becoming scary skinny and prompting multiple calls from concerned neighbors to Child Protective Services.

My parents were obsessed with becoming "pure." They believed purity was the key to accessing divine abilities like moving objects via thought, seeing the Other Side, and communicating mind-to-mind. These divine abilities were part of our everyday lives. My mother screened all calls she received, so if I really needed her to pick up the phone, I'd send a mind-to-mind message first. If I did so, she'd answer right away! Each time I called without the mental communication, it would go straight to the answering machine.

I moved away from home at 17 years old and continued practicing the divine abilities I'd been taught. One weekend, I attended a clairvoyance class at a local crystal shop. I was hoping for a more advanced discussion, but it was only beginner instructions for perceiving beyond the physical senses. The class instructor sensed from my questions that I had a deeper understanding. She pulled me aside later to excitedly say, "You know you're exceptionally gifted, right? I think you're a psychic medium!"

"Isn't everybody?" I replied. Seeing the Other Side was an everyday thing for me by then, and I didn't understand her enthusiasm.

But her comment made me think. As a teenager trying to survive an adult world without any parental support, I needed money. I decided to offer my psychic medium skills on a "by donation only" basis.

I helped people clear their houses of stray souls. I would talk to the dead to arrange signs like songs playing twice in a row or yellow butterflies so that clients could recognize when someone on the Other Side was visiting them. Sometimes my clients wanted me to help them communicate with "anyone who's listening" to get advice.

Connecting to the Other Side is like making a phone call. I can call someone specific, like my lovely grandmother, or I can type random numbers in and just see who picks up. This might be fun for some people but is a terrible idea when you need qualified advice. I began seeing many opportunities to educate the living about boundaries with the dead. Most of my clients were looking for closure with their loved ones. I eventually decided it was against my ethics to accept money from people making decisions clouded by pain, grief, and the complicated emotions that come with communicating with those who have passed on, and I retired from mediumship.

After that, I moved across the country a few times, got married, and opened an online clothing retail company. Quickly realizing that I detest packing and shipping orders but adore standing in someone's closet and helping them figure out how to dress to create the life they want, I pivoted to become a wardrobe mentor. I initially thought my clients would need help sorting out the clothing and accessories that best supported their energy, but I quickly found out that what they actually needed were boundaries. I worked with one woman whose mother-in-law kept buying her clothing two sizes too small to "inspire her" to lose weight. Another client had a partner who would criticize them as "sloppy" if they ever dressed comfortably. One man wanted to wear a kilt to the office but didn't know how to respond to the gross "Are you naked underneath?" remarks from his coworkers. Yet another client had an older sister who kept secretly throwing out their clothes because "It doesn't look good on you."

I gave my clients boundary scripts for how to respond to critical people as well as shopping lists and style guides. My business grew to include an assistant and a sales team. I spoke at a women's conference in Hungary, had clients in seven countries, and hosted my own events. My business was thriving, but my personal life unexpectedly crumbled.

My husband acquired a large amount of secret debt and decided he wanted a divorce. I went from happily married to homeless and alone in a week. In the financial fallout from my divorce, I had to sell off my wardrobe mentoring business. I moved in with a bunch of roommates, got a job at a call center, and all my groceries came from the food bank. It was really rough for almost a year.

Then a friend of a friend reached out with a job offer at her small branding company. I became the director of client services and was responsible for holding our client's hands through their rebrands and website builds. I got a lot of practice setting boundaries with people who thought paying tens of thousands of dollars meant they could change their minds an unlimited amount of times. Nope!

Unfortunately the company went under a short time later, but I'd enjoyed it so much that I decided to become a freelance business consultant. My specialty was heart-centered entrepreneurs like yoga teachers, neuro coaches, angel card readers, and intuitive practitioners. I would travel to my clients' houses and stay for a weekend, a week, or even a month doing a business intensive. I was there to get their website built, set up email and text message marketing systems, create social media posts, and attend conferences to run their sales booths for them.

As it happens, my business consulting clients also really needed boundary help.

"What do I do when my students text me at eleven o'clock at night?" "My husband keeps interrupting my sales call hours because he thinks my business is 'just a little hobby.'" "Someone asked for a refund because they never used the program they bought, but it's been six months since they purchased it. How do I say no nicely?"

I wrote a lot of scripts to help my clients set boundaries with their clients, partners, and friends. I enjoyed this work, but the Universe had other plans for me.

One evening I was chatting with a client and casually mentioned her divine ability to connect and energetically influence others. "I think your gift of connection is quite strong, but it seems like you're only using it a fraction of the time. I bet if you used your gift all of the time, you'd be amazed at the results!"

"Wait. What?" she said.

I was confused that she seemed so surprised. "You know—your divine ability for connection? Your spiritual, intuitive, or energetic gift that allows you to influence other people."

Turns out this was news to her! Because I'd grown up in a family that used divine abilities all the time, it was so basic in my mind that I often forgot it was unfamiliar to most people. She asked me to make a list of her top divine abilities that I had observed. I included how strong the abilities were on a scale from 1 to 10 and what percentage of the time she was using them.

She called me back later that week to make a similar divine abilities list for her son. Then she referred a friend to me to get a similar list, who then got a list for her spouse. Within a few weeks, I had more demand for my divine abilities lists than I did for business consulting!

I wrote a master list of the top 60 divine abilities and released it as a free pdf to anyone who joined the Facebook group I created to help people learn more. Over the next two years, that Facebook group grew to hundreds of people, and I became a full-time spiritual teacher. I certified and trained 23 coaches in identifying people's divine abilities. I taught weekly online workshops on energy work, how to connect with your GUHP (my acronym for God/Goddess, Universe, or Higher Power), and how to identify who's in your entourage of angels, animal guides, ancestors, or other supportive beings following you around 24/7. My most popular workshops (with quadruple the sales) were about setting boundaries, especially what to say when people criticize your "woo-woo" beliefs.

Simultaneously, I was in therapy working through my childhood wounds. At the end of 2019, I was on my therapist's couch, wrapped in a fuzzy blanket, and had the shattering epiphany that the main reason I felt compelled to be a spiritual teacher was an attempt to undo the harm I went through as a little kid by "saving" my students, which I realized isn't possible.

I knew I had to quit.

I closed down the Facebook group, sold off parts of my intellectual property to one of my students, and stopped being a spiritual teacher. It doesn't matter to me how much money I can make or the number of people I can help if I'm only doing it to soothe an open emotional wound. I was replaying old hurt instead of actually healing, so I needed to do something else unrelated to my childhood trauma.

I started 2020 not sure exactly what I would do, but I knew I was tired of working only online for the last two years and wanted to focus on hosting in-person local events. I wish I could insert a laugh track right here because of how ridiculously awful that plan worked out for global pandemic reasons. I ended up spending 2020 staying home, pulling weeds in the backyard, and considering the patterns of my career up to that point.

I began to realize:

- When I was a psychic medium, I taught boundaries between the living and the dead.
- When I was a wardrobe mentor, I taught boundaries for people with clothing critics.
- When I was a business consultant, I taught boundaries to help my clients with their clients.
- When I was a spiritual teacher, I taught boundaries to my students for when family members didn't understand their beliefs.

Teaching boundaries has been a common theme my whole life!

At the beginning of 2021, I decided to take the hint from the Universe and officially became a boundary coach. I started on TikTok, telling stories about saying the thing and grew my account to a few hundred thousand followers with several videos reaching almost 2 million views. I coached clients across the United States and Canada, and a few in Europe. I created custom boundary training for businesses, nonprofits, and universities. I shared my collection of favorite boundary phrases as flash cards.

Furthering my path to self-discovery, in February 2022, I got the good news that I'm autistic. I felt surprised yet delighted by this diagnosis because it explained why most of my boundary coaching clients are neurodivergent. Like attracts like!

I think a lot of my professional success is due to being autistic. I have amazing pattern recognition for language, human behavior has always been a special interest, and I'm naturally a direct communicator. As I relaxed into my diagnosis, I shifted my business to better meet my needs. The work I do is important, and the best way for me to accomplish that work is to take really good care of myself and my community.

I take a nap most days. I check in with my best friend and business collaborator every day. I hired a wonderful person to monitor my social media comments and share only the happy or helpful ones with me. I stopped offering one-to-one coaching at the beginning of 2023 to make space for one-to-many coaching. I created a weekly email newsletter so I could share my thoughts in a longer format, because I prefer to explain things fully. I wrote this book.

Over the years, I've learned a lot about who I am and how I got to the place I am now in my life. I'm a fat, queer, autistic, white, cisgender woman. I value safety and compassion. I have an eclectic, self-taught background. And I'm passionate about helping others learn to say the thing. Why?

The world is changing quickly. We are facing a storm of societal selfishness. It's billionaires, corporations, politicians, celebrities, and people picking the wants of the one over the needs of the many. They are bold without hesitation. But guess what? We can be bold without hesitation too.

We can speak up in defense of ourselves and others. We can set boundaries. We can add our voices to the revolution for a kinder, more inclusive world.

We can say the thing.

I think the best way to learn communication skills is to communicate in person. In an ideal situation, I would invite you over to my place, where we could spend the afternoon together surrounded by my dozens of house plants. I'd give you a choice of fuzzy blankets. We'd have plenty of time to sit on the couch and talk.

I'd tell you the story of how I became a boundary coach. I'd ask who in your childhood had the power to say what was okay and what was not okay. At some point, we'd get hungry and move to sit at the table.

While eating lunch, I'd pull out a piece of paper and a pen to draw for you the boundary scripts I use in public versus in private. We'd dive into the challenges you've personally had with saying the thing.

Maybe you're ADHD and need a response to your family telling you, "Just try harder!" Or you're fat and want a comeback to your coworker's food policing. Perhaps you have a neighbor who makes so-called jokes about racial stereotypes. Whatever the issue, I'd flip the paper over and write down for you a dozen script options.

As the sun goes down, you'd go home with a full belly, a plant cutting to propagate, and several pages filled with my round handwriting. You'd know how to say the thing.

The closest I can get to hosting you like that for a one-to-one educational afternoon is through this book. Wherever you may be reading this, I invite you to grab a fuzzy blanket, maybe a snack or two, and let's talk!

PART I

BOUNDARIES
& HOW TO
SET THEM

The
4 Boundary
Choices

Snip, snip, snip.

Matteo's shoulders scrunched around his ears.

Snip, snip.

He closed his eyes in frustration.

Snip . . . snip. SNIP!

Shaking out his clenched fists, he grabbed his water bottle and stepped out of his cubicle to take a break in the workplace kitchen. He hurried past his coworker's desk, deliberately not looking at the scattering of fingernail clipping "confetti" all over the floor.

As a pre-lunch ritual each day, Matteo's coworker cuts their fingernails at their desk while Matteo seethes in the adjoining cubicle. The day before our boundary coaching session, he'd found a fingernail clipping shard stuck to the hem of his pants when he removed his shoes after work!

"I hate my coworker," Matteo told me over the phone. "I hate my coworker, and I'm going to quit this job if they don't stop clipping their fingernails at their desk."

"What did your coworker say when you asked them to stop?" I asked.

"Oh, I've never said anything to them. They should already know it's not okay to cut their nails at work."

"What would happen if you said to them, 'Hey, I found a piece of your fingernail stuck to my pants yesterday. Will you please cut your nails in the restroom or at home from now on?'" I said.

"Well, I don't want to be a jerk about it," Matteo grumbled.

"Okay," I replied. "What if you asked, 'Hey, I've noticed you cut your nails at your desk every day. What's up with that?'"

"Yeah. I could say that. Do you think they would take the hint and stop clipping their fingernails at work?"

"I don't know," I said, truthfully. "But I encourage you to say the thing and find out!"

The next day at work, Matteo took a deep breath and stepped into the office kitchen, where his coworker was pouring coffee.

"So," he began. "Why do you always clip your nails at lunch?"

With raised eyebrows, Matteo's coworker turned toward him.

"What? How did you know I clip my nails at lunch?"

"Your nail clippers are kind of noisy," Matteo replied.

"Oh no!" said his coworker. "I've been eating oranges at lunch, and the rinds get stuck under my nails when I peel them, so I cut my nails first to prevent that. I had no idea you could hear me clipping my nails every day!"

"Maybe you could clip your nails at home before coming to work?"

"No, I know I'd forget. I'll just stop bringing oranges for lunch or peel them before I pack them or something. I'm sorry if my nail clipping bothered you."

"Yeah, no worries," said Matteo with a shrug. "Oh! Is that fresh coffee?"

The conversation moved on, and, as far as I know, his coworker never clipped their nails at their desk again.

As Matteo learned in the above situation, there are four choices when setting boundaries:

1. **Silence**
2. **Extremes**
3. **Direct communication**
4. **Indirect communication**

When his coworker's daily fingernail-cutting ritual began, Matteo's first choice was silence.

Why didn't he say anything? Feelings! Lots and lots of uncomfortable feelings. Matteo felt:

- Shocked that someone would do personal grooming at their desk
- Hopeful they would just stop after a few days
- Unsure about what to say because he had never been in a situation like this before
- Scared of being labeled a "jerk"
- Afraid his coworker would be upset with him if confronted
- Worried that he'd waited too long to speak up

His next choice was resorting to extremes. By the time we had our boundary coaching session, he had updated his resume and was starting to search for new jobs. He was willing to quit to get away from his annoying coworker. Why? Again, uncomfortable feelings! Matteo felt:

- Furious at his coworker
- Hopelessly trapped in a sensory nightmare
- Resentful that his boss hadn't done anything about the fingernail clipping "confetti" being spread throughout the office

During our coaching session, I first encouraged Matteo to try direct communication before upending his life by quitting a job that he otherwise really liked. He disagreed; plainly asking his coworker to stop cutting their nails at their desk felt too unfamiliar and risky.

After talking through his feelings with me, Matteo ultimately chose indirect communication. We role-played several possible scripts, and he picked what felt the most natural to him. It worked!

In my experience, all four boundary choices can be the best option in some scenarios but an ineffective option in others. None of them are inherently "wrong," but they are all a choice.

Silence is first on the list, because it's the most common boundary choice I see people make. There's often the assumption that choosing silence is a way to "not choose," but it doesn't work like that. For example, not replying to a text message is still sending a message, albeit a silent one.

It's okay to choose silence! You can say, "Oh, excuse me," and walk out of the room. You can cross to the other side of the street. You can block their social media profile. You can change your schedule to not bump into them anymore at the store or gym. Those are all fine choices to make.

If you tend to choose silence, please consider if you're choosing it because it's the best option in a given situation or if it's because you're uncomfortable with the other choices. I'll discuss this more when we cover why people struggle with boundaries.

Extremes are the opposite end of the boundary choices spectrum. If silence is doing nothing, saying nothing, and avoiding, extremes are doing everything, saying everything, and confronting!

Extremes are often accompanied with intense emotions. This is when we quit the job, end the relationship, call the police, move out of the apartment, march in the streets, burn it down, and get noisy about it!

Extremes can be the best choice when someone has completely crossed the line. It's okay to choose a big response when something really not okay has happened. There is a time and a place to protest in the biggest, loudest way.

If you tend to choose extremes, please consider if it's because you tried everything else but it hasn't worked. Or if you're swinging to an extreme as your first choice before even communicating, like how Matteo wanted to quit his job but hadn't attempted asking his coworker to stop clipping their fingernails yet.

If you're unaware of the four boundary choices, it's common to choose silence for as long as you can, avoiding the issue, and then when you just can't take it anymore, jump to extremes! I highly encourage you to try the middle choices first: direct and indirect communication.

Direct communication is to the point. Saying what you mean in the most straightforward way possible. You don't need additional clues to interpret the message. This can take longer because all the relevant details are included and clarified.

In anthropology, this type of communication happens in "low-context cultures." Low-context cultures are those that communicate information in direct, explicit, and precise ways. If there is context needed so the message is clear, it's spoken aloud instead of assuming everyone already knows. There are often fewer nonverbal cues that could be interpreted multiple ways. The most polite thing to do in a low-context culture is to ask in a straightforward manner and not make someone guess what you want. Examples of low-context cultures include the majority of autistic and

ADHD people, the deaf community, New Yorkers, Germany, and Scandinavian countries.

Indirect communication is implying your meaning. To understand your message, the other person relies on clues previously shared between you or within your group. These clues might be vocal tone, body language, timing, social status, relationship history, etc.

Known as "high-context cultures" in anthropology, these groups communicate in implicit ways: meaning is implied instead of directly stated. You don't have to say everything out loud because everyone already knows what's being referenced without the explanation. The most polite thing you can do in a high-context culture is to pre-emptively guess what someone wants and not make them ask directly. Examples include intimate relationships with lots of shared history, like long-term friends, partners, or families, as well as small towns and shared interest groups. Communities of Jewish, Arab, Chinese, or Korean people can also be considered high-context cultures for their traditions of politeness, hospitality, and family loyalty.

If I say to you, "Please pass me the blue butter dish that's in front of you on the table," it is very clear what I want. If I pick up my butter knife and begin opening my bread roll, then pause and make eye contact with you, I'm expecting you to guess that I'd like you to pass me the butter dish.

There are many benefits to both choices. Indirect communication can make people already in a group feel a sense of belonging and is potentially really fast when everyone knows all the clues. You can have a whole conversation with an eyebrow raise and flick of a finger! Direct communication is ideal for including diverse perspectives in a conversation and being exquisitely clear about what is being shared.

As a boundary coach, I often talk to frustrated individuals who are upset their boundaries aren't being respected. My client Alice was super annoyed that her sister Tamara kept feeding human food to Alice's dog, Sneezy.

"Did you tell Tamara to stop giving Sneezy little bits of pizza?" I asked her.

"I did! I said 'Sneezy gets gassy when he eats cheese.'"

"Hmm. What else did you say?"

"I told her that the vet said Sneezy is too chunky for his breed," Alice replied.

"Okay," I continued. "Did you clearly and directly say, 'Tamara, I know you like giving Sneezy treats when he begs, but it's not okay to feed him pizza anymore. It's hurting him. If you want to give him something, there's a bag of dog treats in the cupboard by the leashes.'"

"Not in those words. But Tamara knows what I meant! She knows Sneezy shouldn't be eating pizza!"

"Before we assume Tamara definitely knows to not ever give Sneezy human food again and she's doing it anyway because she doesn't care about his health, I invite you to talk to her one more time."

I wrote Alice a script to text Tamara about Sneezy. Tamara replied she didn't think a few bites of pizza were "a big deal" but if Alice was going to "make a fuss" about it, Tamara would give dog treats only to Sneezy from now on. Alice counted that as a boundary win!

Please consider if you're making the same mistake Alice was about assuming you're choosing direct communication when actually you're being indirect. Indirect communication was "Sneezy gets gassy when he eats cheese" and direct communication was "Do not give cheese to Sneezy."

To some people, those sentences have the same meaning of "No more cheese for the dog." Others wouldn't have ever realized that "Sneezy gets gassy" was a boundary being set without the additional context from Alice.

This is why direct communication is my favorite of the four boundary choices. It's the clearest, most effective way to communicate your boundaries with the majority of people.

What Are Boundaries & Why Do We Struggle with Them?

WHAT IS A BOUNDARY?

A boundary is a communicated expression of what is okay and what is not okay.

By my definition, a stop sign is a boundary. A NO TRESPASSING sign on a fence is a boundary. Shaking your head to indicate no is a boundary. Putting your hand up in a stop gesture is a boundary. Texting someone and saying, "Hey, I'm not interested in continuing this conversation," is a boundary.

Anytime and any way you communicate "I'm okay with this" or "I'm not okay with that" is a boundary. This is an intentionally broad definition because I want you to take a step back from the idea that a boundary has to be this big, scary, dramatic thing or that we only set boundaries when something has gone terribly wrong or someone is upset.

Boundaries can and often are a gentle, casual, normal part of our everyday accommodation of human relationships.

For example, I called my friend Blaise several weeks ago. As we were chatting, he said, "I don't like when you call me without texting first to ask if you can call now. I know that you just want to chat, but it gets my adrenaline going."

Blaise has had a lot of life-changing phone calls in his life, the kind where one call overturns everything you thought you knew and leaves you reeling. He told me, "I hate sudden phone calls. From now on, would you ask me first via text and say, 'Hey are you available for a call?' and wait for me to reply before calling me?"

That's a boundary. It was calm. It was kind. It was not a big deal. Now, I always text first before calling Blaise. Easy-peasy, no problem.

Let's extend the example and imagine it wasn't easy-peasy for me to text him first before calling. Maybe that doesn't fit with my schedule or how my brain works or any other reason. It's totally okay for him to ask for what he needs—a heads-up before a phone call—and I could then ask for what I needed—a way to call without texting first—and together we'd figure it out.

Maybe he'd always call me first. Maybe we'd pre-schedule our calls so Blaise knew what time to expect me to ring his phone. Maybe we'd switch to an asynchronous video chat app instead of calls. Whatever worked best for both of us.

Part of having relationships is doing what we can to make life a bit easier for one another. Setting boundaries by sharing what is okay and not okay with you helps the people in your life better support you and you support them. It doesn't need to be a fight. Boundaries can be a calm conversation between people working together to meet one another's needs. Humans are social creatures. We are the dominant cooperative species on the planet. Boundaries are the limits and expectations that help us exist harmoniously together: what is okay in your space, what is okay in my space, and how those spaces intersect.

WHY DO PEOPLE STRUGGLE WITH BOUNDARIES?

It's much easier for everyone to exist together when we have boundaries, so why is it such a struggle? Why do some people feel like boundaries are always a big, scary, dramatic thing? There are three main reasons.

1. You Don't Want to Be a Jerk

At some point in your childhood, you probably experienced someone who was physically bigger, louder, and angrier than you. Someone who had the most power in the room and set all the limits. They might not have used the word *boundaries*, but it was clear that they got to say what was okay and not okay because they had more size, volume, intensity, and access to resources than anyone else around.

This description might immediately bring one or more people to your mind. It might've been a playground bully, a caretaker or parent, a teacher, or an athletic coach. Maybe you don't recall anyone specific, but you're probably familiar with this "might makes right" archetype. Where I'm from, we refer to people like this as jerks.

This is why the most common answer I get for the question, "Why didn't you set a boundary?" is:

"Oh, I just didn't want to be a jerk."

"I don't want to be a jerk about it."

"It seemed like a jerk thing to do."

Many people associate saying "I'm okay with this" or "I'm not okay with that" with jerks. When you say how you feel and ask for what you want, a little voice screams, "Nooo! We're being like that jerk! That big, loud, angry, has-the-most-power-in-the-room jerk!" Then you don't say the thing, set the boundary, or speak up because you didn't like how it felt when that person or people did that to you.

At this moment, I'm gently inviting you to be willing to let that fear go. If good, kind people like you don't set boundaries because you believe that's jerk behavior, then the only people who will keep setting limits are the jerks!

Consider separating what that jerk did from how they did it. It's really understandable that you felt hurt when someone bigger, louder, angrier, and who had more power than you told you what you could or could not do. It might've felt scary or overwhelming. You might've felt that you didn't have a choice.

You aren't being a jerk if you set boundaries, as long as you communicate clearly, directly, and kindly. It's okay to ask for what you want and need.

Unfortunately, you're not the only one who might've learned that setting limits is a jerk thing to do. Many people don't yet know how to separate the part that's okay (asking for what you want) from the part that's not okay (bullying others because you have more power than them).

When you go out into the big, wild world and set boundaries, you'll bump into people who are offended by you saying how you feel and asking for what you want. They may have experienced limits and boundaries only from big, loud, angry jerks and lump you into that category.

It's a new experience for them when you come along and communicate your boundary in a kind, direct way.

Until they're open to learning otherwise, they probably will perceive all boundary setting as jerk behavior. I encourage you to keep setting boundaries anyway because while they might not appreciate it at the moment, in the long run it's helping them and you to have better relationships. Their reaction or even accusation of you being a jerk doesn't mean that you are one.

2. You Don't Want to Make It Worse

The second reason you might struggle with boundaries is you don't want to make the situation worse.

I frequently hear, "If I say, 'Hey, that's not okay,' it's going to make it worse."

Let's pause for a moment and explore that assumption. Imagine a roommate or partner borrows your hoodie without asking and returns it with mustard stains down the front. You say to them, "Please ask me before borrowing my clothes," or "If you wear my hoodie and spill something on it, please wash it before returning it to my closet." What happens next?

A reasonable person will respond with something like, "Thank you for telling me. I won't do that again."

Or, "Oh! I'm sorry. I didn't realize I spilled mustard on it. I'll wash that now and be sure I ask first next time I borrow your hoodie."

Maybe, "I really love wearing that hoodie, and you're usually not around when I want to put it on. It feels like too much of a hassle to check with you each time, so I'm going to buy my own identical hoodie so I can stop borrowing yours. What brand is it?"

Even, "Huh. That's a change from our previous open-closet policy. Is the issue that I borrowed it without checking first or that it was dirty when I put it back? Can we talk more about how we lend clothes between us and who is responsible for what household laundry?"

When told a boundary, reasonable people will express gratitude, accept the feedback, take accountability, make an action plan to avoid repeating the problem, and/or ask clarifying questions.

An unreasonable person will **DARVO**: deny, attack, and reverse victim and offender. Psychologist Jennifer Freyd created this acronym to identify the reaction pattern of perpetrators of wrongdoing when they're held accountable for their behavior.

- **Denying:** "I didn't spill mustard on the hoodie!"
- **Attacking:** "You always blame me for stains on your clothes."
- **Reversing Victim and Offender:** "You spilled hot chocolate on the couch last week and just flipped the cushion over instead of cleaning it up. Instead of blaming me for mystery mustard stains, maybe you should start taking responsibility for all the messes you make. It's your fault our house is such a dump. I can't even talk to you when you get like this. You're such a jerk!"

If you've ever had an unreasonable person DARVO you, it is understandable that you'd hesitate to set boundaries again after that bad experience. It is common human behavior to avoid repeating an action that hurt you the last time you did it.

If your struggle with boundaries is that you don't want to make the situation worse, you've probably experienced at some point that saying the thing did make a situation worse. Having someone deny it happened, attack you instead, and make themselves the victim and you the offender when they were the one who did something wrong is definitely worse.

I also want you to know that DARVOing is something only unreasonable people do. Are you hesitant to say the thing because you assume everyone will DARVO if you express how you feel and ask for what you want? Has the person you want to set boundaries with DARVOed you in the past? Or are they generally a reasonable, lovely, and kind person, and you're projecting what happened before on what's happening now? Is it safe for you to set boundaries with this person? You're the expert on your situation and ultimately know what is best for you.

3. You Don't Want to Upset Anyone

The third reason you might struggle with boundaries is because you don't want to upset anyone.

Let's take a moment to acknowledge that "I just don't want to upset anyone" is a tender-hearted motivation. Most likely you're someone who feels deeply. You really love and care about people. You want them to be happy!

It's different from not wanting to be a jerk. Not wanting to be a jerk is about how you're being perceived by others. Not wanting to upset anyone is about how other people are feeling. It is a very loving intention.

Unfortunately, not saying the thing might come from a loving place but can still hurt people. When you don't tell people what's okay and what's not okay, you're setting them up to fail. If you want to show them how much you love them, the most loving thing you can do is to set them up to succeed.

For example, my partner (whom I will hereafter refer to as Sexy Beast) and I were cuddling on their couch the other night. I noticed a tiny piece of white fuzzy lint in their beard. I reached my hand up to their face to pick it off, but before I could, Sexy Beast flinched sharply backward.

I said, "Oh! Are you okay with me touching your facial hair?"

"Actually, I'm not," Sexy Beast replied. "It really irritates my dry skin, it tickles a bit, and I would prefer you didn't."

"Okay! You have a bit of lint in your beard," I said helpfully.

And now I know not to touch their face like that.

It seems like a very small thing to ask someone not to touch your facial hair, but setting and respecting even small boundaries will build trust in a relationship.

Sexy Beast knows they can say no to me, and I will respond in a reasonable way and respect their boundaries. I feel confident Sexy Beast will tell me when bigger problems happen in the future because they communicated a small problem in a kind, direct way today.

This makes our relationship better. It builds trust. It builds love. It helps us set each other up for success.

What might the other option have been? I could have kept touching Sexy Beast's facial hair for however long. They would have kept flinching and hating how it tickled. Then they would have become irritated, building secret resentment like an underground volcano until they can't take it anymore and erupt angrily the next time I reach over to dab a bit of spaghetti sauce off their chin at lunch.

"Ahh! Stop touching my face! I hate it!"

"I've touched your face a million times. Why didn't you ever say anything before?"

"I didn't want to upset you."

"I get that, but now I'm worried that I can't trust you to tell me when there's a small problem before it becomes a big issue."

Thankfully, Sexy Beast is the type of person to say how they feel and ask for what they want. They told me to not touch their facial hair, and now I don't.

It is a loving, generous thing to set boundaries and say, "Hey, this is what's okay and this is what's not okay." It doesn't have to be a scary, dramatic moment. If you're concerned about upsetting people, I celebrate your tender-hearted impulse, and I invite you to set your loved ones up to succeed by saying the thing.

PART II

BOUNDARY SCRIPTS TO HELP YOU SAY THE THING

How to Use Boundary Scripts

I've only traveled outside of the United States once, when I flew to Budapest, Hungary, to keynote speak at a women's conference. I do not speak Hungarian and didn't realize until I landed in Budapest that I couldn't easily use Google Translate on my phone without cell service.

I wandered around the airport asking, "Excuse me. Do you speak English?" until I found someone to help me exchange my money, get in a safe taxi, and tell the driver my destination.

It would've been a lot faster if I had memorized the Hungarian phrases for:

- Where is the money exchange?
- Where is the taxi queue?
- Here is where I'm going. How much for you to drive me there?

It was an amazing experience staying at a grand old hotel on an island in the Danube River, eating gelato shaped like a rose, and connecting with incredible women from across Europe. However, I learned that any future travels need to include memorizing, or at least writing down, some basic phrases in the local language.

If you're new to saying the thing, setting boundaries for yourself can feel as confusing as traveling somewhere you don't speak the language. The wonderful news is that you don't have to be fluent to enjoy your travels. Similar to bringing along local language scripts to ask, "Which way to the train station?" this part of the book includes three scripts so you'll know how to respond in any boundary setting scenario.

Oftentimes, other people who teach boundaries will separate their boundary scripts by relationship type: what to say to your partner, parents, friends, coworkers, neighbors, etc.

For me, the boundary script I'd say to my best friend, my sister, or my partner is the same when I'm speaking with one of them in private and different from what I'd say out in public. It's private versus public that changes how I communicate my boundaries, not the person I'm communicating with, so it makes more sense to me to separate boundary scripts by setting instead of by relationship type.

The three boundary scripts covered in the following pages are Public Now, Private Now, and Private Later.

The Public Now Script is best for quick interactions, like when you choose to say the thing to someone you're not emotionally close to and/or there are other people around. I use this script online, especially on social media, or with strangers when I'm out and about.

The Private Now Script is for longer one-to-one conversations, where you're saying the thing to someone whose feelings you care about, you need to have a good working relationship with them, or if it's a sensitive, handle-with-care topic.

This is the one I use most often of the three and is how I say the thing to my friends, partners, siblings, work team, and loved ones. My boundary students get great results using this script with children, bosses, coworkers, employees, neighbors, teachers, parents, and in-laws.

The Private Later Script is for returning to have a one-to-one conversation after time has passed. I use this script with my loved ones and with therapists, doctors, and anyone I have an uneven power dynamic with. With sensitive conversations, I often need time to feel my feelings and think through how I want to respond before going back to that person and saying the thing.

The next pages go into the above scripts in more detail. Please note that all relationships are different. How and with whom you use the scripts will differ. Just because I use them one way doesn't mean a different choice is "wrong." Trust yourself!

PUBLIC NOW SCRIPT:
Disrupter, Statement, Transition

Waiting in line outside to order at my favorite sandwich shop, I sunflowered my face to the sun and breathed in the summer air. In the colder months, the Salt Lake Valley is clogged with gross inversion, so I appreciate the clear days in June. The neighborhood is decorated with rainbow flags to celebrate Pride Month, I'm about to get some delicious food, and I'm having a great day.

Unfortunately, the person behind me in the line is not having a great day. They interpreted my sun-facing stance, angled slightly toward them, as an invitation to start a conversation by saying, "Ugh. Don't you just hate all these gay flags?"

Startled, I said the first thing that popped into my queer brain. "Hmm. I am not the right person for you to share that with."

Then I turned my back toward them, ending the conversation. I refused to let their bigotry ruin my day!

To respond to that stranger, I used the Public Now Script, which has three parts:

> **Disrupter:** *Hmm.*
> **Statement:** *I am not the right person for you to share that with.*
> **Transition:** *Turning my back.*

I recommend the Public Now Script when you choose to say the thing in "public," or anytime it's not a private one-to-one conversation, and you're responding to something they said or did right in that moment, a.k.a. "now." It is primarily for quick interactions and not long conversations. Sometimes when setting boundaries, it's okay to keep it short and to the point.

This script is used most often with strangers, people you're not emotionally close with, or people you have a supervisory role toward, like if you're a trail guide and you're responsible for safely directing tourists along the edge of the Grand Canyon.

> **Disrupter:** *Nope!*
> **Statement:** *Get back on this side of the fence. That side is off limits.*
> **Transition:** *Come look at this map instead!*

Here's more detail about the three parts of the Public Now Script:

THE DISRUPTER

The Disrupter breaks, interrupts, or "disrupts" the flow of the conversation. I imagine it like those little stop signs that crossing guards hold at crosswalks to signal to drivers they need to wait for pedestrians. The conversation is going along, going along, going along, until someone suddenly says, "Stop!"

Using a Disrupter gives you a way to signal, "There is a problem. I'm not okay with what you just said or did!" What I call Disrupters are parts of speech known as *emotive interjections*. Here are 20 examples:

1.	Hey	11.	Ope
2.	No	12.	Oh no
3.	Stop	13.	Nah
4.	Oh	14.	Alrighty
5.	Um	15.	Oops
6.	Wow	16.	Ouch
7.	Uh-uh	17.	Whoops
8.	Hold up	18.	Yeah
9.	Eww	19.	Ugh
10.	Yikes	20.	Hmm

Note: Most profanity can also be used as Disrupters, but I'm sure you already know those options!

You can mix and match any Disrupters that feel comfortable. Most people have one or two that they use frequently. The Disrupters that come most quickly and naturally for me are "hey" and "ope."

Examples of Disruptors in Use:

"Ope! Please back up a bit; that's too close for me. Thanks!"

"Hey! I don't need an explanation; this is my area of expertise."

A friend of mine says "wow" as her most frequent Disrupter. "Wow. I hope you're not saying that to me because you think I agree with you. Because I don't."

My favorite I-wouldn't-say-it-but-I-am-glad-it-exists-in-the-world Disrupter I've ever heard from a boundary student was "barf!" When I asked them to use it in a sentence, they replied with the following example:

"Barf. What a misogynistic thing to say. Don't ever repeat that to me again, or I'm going straight to the human resources department!"

THE STATEMENT

The Statement is the boundary, limit, accommodation, or request that you're communicating.

Here are 12 examples:

1. Please don't comment on my weight.
2. I prefer you not do that again.
3. I don't like that.
4. Stop asking me.
5. Don't touch my wheelchair.
6. I'm not comfortable with that type of language. Please stop.
7. I'm not a hugger. Please back off.
8. I don't need help with this. I've got it.
9. That's not okay.
10. I'm not going to answer questions about that.
11. That's not something I'm available for.
12. Please don't eat my fries.

THE TRANSITION

The Transition is how you move forward after the Statement. If I say to you, "Oh, please don't ask me about work right now. That's a messy topic. Let's talk about you, though! How is your new puppy?" The "Let's talk about you, though!" and asking an unrelated question is the Transition.

Transitions are so helpful, both as part of the Public Now Script and on their own. I was once in an Uber when the driver made an offensive comment about "female drivers." I felt unsafe and uncomfortable with his aggressive attitude, but since I was almost to my destination, I decided to transition the conversation by saying:

"Oh! Speaking of women . . . are you married?"

He said, "Yes."

"Where is your wife from?"

"She's from here."

"Oh, I love living here! It's been tough to get my garden to grow, though. Do you garden?"

He did! And he spent the remainder of the ride telling me all about his honeydew melons and how proud he was that they turned out super juicy, which is incredibly difficult to accomplish in the desert where we live.

With Public Now Scripts, you're not trying to have a conversation about the Statement. Your goal is to move forward or leave.

I strongly suggest picking one or two Transitions that you like and memorizing them! My favorites are "Excuse me" paired with walking away and "I wanted to ask you about [an unrelated topic]." My go-to unrelated topics are pets, gardening, and the weather. Other good options include local events, sports teams, and upcoming holidays.

Here are five *leave-the-conversation* Transition examples.

1. Thanks!
2. Excuse me.
3. Appreciate it!
4. I've got to go now.
5. Good-bye.

Here are five *topic-switch* Transition examples:

1. Let's talk about something else.
2. Let's change the subject.
3. Let's lighten it up and talk about something fun now!
4. I've been meaning to ask you about [fill in the blank].
5. Speaking of that, [ask an unrelated question]?

Here are five *nonverbal* Transition examples:

1. Walking away
2. Silence
3. Cold stare
4. High-five
5. Turning away

PUT THE
PUBLIC NOW SCRIPT
TOGETHER

If you regularly encounter situations where someone is making a comment to you in public and you need an immediate response, I encourage you to take a moment now to mix and match your favorite Disrupters, Statements, and Transitions to create your own Public Now boundary scripts.

Here are five examples to get you started:

Disrupter	Statement	Transition
Oh!	Please don't put any salad on my plate. I'm allergic to carrots.	Thanks anyway!
Hey,	That was not funny; that was offensive.	Excuse me. [walk away]
Nope.	I am not the right person for you to share that with.	I'm going to go now.
Hmm.	I am not comfortable with this topic.	Can we talk about something else?
Yikes!	We don't talk about people's bodies like that.	Knock it off!

PRIVATE NOW SCRIPT:
Behavior, Intention, Impact, Behavior

I was walking on the riverside trail with my friend Binky, and she was telling me about an autistic child that she knows.

"They're only a little bit autistic, but it's enough to make them really good at math and puzzles."

"Hmm. May I share something with you that it sounds like you might not know? About how you just described that child?" I asked.

"Sure!" said Binky. "I always learn something new from you when we hang out."

"When you said that they are 'only a little bit autistic,' I know your intention was to compliment their amazing mathematical skills. Unfortunately, it perpetuates harmful stereotypes to describe the autism spectrum that way.

"People assume the spectrum is like a 1-to-10 scale, where some people are only a 2 out of 10 autistic, and others are a 9 out of 10 autistic! That's not how it works.

"Autism is a spectrum like a rainbow. Even when it's hard to see the green stripe, it doesn't mean it's not there. You might not be able to see all of someone's autistic traits, but that doesn't make them more or less autistic.

"A better way to say it would be 'They are autistic and have a special interest in math and puzzles.'"

Through my whole explanation, Binky and I had continued walking down the trail and now we paused under a tree to enjoy the shade for a minute.

"Thank you for sharing that with me, Kami. I'm going to say it differently from now on."

"Thank you for being willing to listen! Now, what were you saying about this autistic kid that you know?"

When giving feedback to Binky, I used the Private Now Script which has four parts:

Behavior:
Describe what they did or said that's not okay.
When you said that they are "only a little bit autistic."

Intention:
Share what you're assuming their positive intent is.
I know your intention was to compliment their amazing mathematical skills!

Impact:
Share the harmful impact they had.
Unfortunately, it perpetuates harmful stereotypes to describe the autism spectrum that way.

Behavior:
Describe what they could do or say that is okay
A better way to say it would be "they are autistic and have a special interest in math and puzzles."

The Private Now Script is best for setting boundaries in a private one-to-one conversation. It's much longer than the Public Now Script and can be used as the beginning of a more nuanced discussion that might include clarification questions, expressing feelings, apologies, and more.

Think of it like a four-ingredient sandwich.

The Behavior descriptions are a pair of bread slices on each end. Intentions are the peanut butter holding it together. The Impact is the messy raspberry jam leaking out everywhere!

Ready to break it down further?

THE BEHAVIOR THEY DID

If you recall, a boundary is a communicated expression of what is okay and what is not okay. In the Private Now Script, the first description of Behavior is where you clearly describe what happened that was not okay with you. Most of the time, this part starts with the phrase "when you."

For example, "When you stood up really fast, I know you were just in a hurry to greet Darrell, but you accidentally stepped on my foot and kicked my walker over. Will you please be more mindful next time?"

The "When you stood up really fast" part is the first Behavior description, the first slice of bread to begin building the sandwich. It's important to be as clear as possible with your description of their behavior. Skip vague language like, "when you did that" or "when you said that" because while you know what "that" is referring to, they may not. Do your best to factually and calmly state only the behavior that happened.

THEIR INTENTION

Why did they do or say that?

The Intention part of the Private Now Script isn't about knowing for sure people's reasons. Just make your best guess. If it's a toss-up between "they're awful and trying to hurt me" and "they're ignorant and didn't know what would happen," I invite you to choose the most generous possibility.

Assume their intention was to be helpful. Funny. Clever. Curious. Friendly. It won't hurt anything and often helps smooth everything over if you give someone the benefit of the doubt. Humans like to be thought well of. With a few rare exceptions, people will claim positive intentions if you suggest them.

The vast majority of people aren't cartoon villains singing songs about how happy they are to be evil. They think they are doing a good thing, even if the impact of their choice is harmful.

The more you practice assuming positive intentions in others, the better you'll get at identifying their motivations. If you say out loud the good part they were trying to accomplish, people usually agree and then will be much more open to the boundary you're setting with them.

THE IMPACT

What was the end result? What outcome was achieved? What are the consequences of our choices?

In the Private Now Script, the Impact part is when you tell the other person that despite their good intentions, harm has occurred. This is when you outline the ways you or others have gotten hurt and how that feels.

This often begins with the word or the dismayed tone of "unfortunately . . ." because you're giving them bummer news:

"Unfortunately, it didn't turn out the way we'd hoped."

"I wish I didn't have to tell you that the results weren't good."

"Sadly, it hurt more than it helped."

Don't shame or guilt them. This isn't about making them feel bad; the goal here is to inform them of the outcome of their words or actions. In my experience, most people will be dismayed to learn that their good intentions didn't result in the impact they were trying to have. Some people even express gratitude to learn this information!

THE BEHAVIOR YOU WANT

The second description of Behavior is for saying what you do want to have happen in the future. This is the boundary portion of the script where you ask for what you want or need.

The clearer you are with your instructions, the more likely you'll get the results you want. If you're vague, the other person has to guess what you're looking for. Imagine you're giving directions; there is a big difference between "go west" and "travel three days west, turn left at the river, and it's the red brick house with the broken porch swing." Be as precise as you can.

I find it helpful to say, "In the future" or "from now on" when I say this part of the Private Now Script, but if those aren't turns of phrase you use, it's okay to leave them off.

PUTTING THE PRIVATE NOW
SCRIPT TOGETHER

Here are ten examples to get you started in writing your own

Behavior	Intention	Impact	Behavior
When you grab stuff out of my hands while I'm on my crutches,	I know your intention is to help me.	Unfortunately that can cause me to become unbalanced and fall over, which is really dangerous!	Please ask me if I need help carrying anything before grabbing stuff.
I think when you say, "Here comes the chubby monkey!" to Mally,	your intention is to be the loving grandfather I know you are.	But because she has brown skin, it sounds like you're making a comment about her race when you compare her to a monkey.	In the future, please stick with greetings like, "Here comes Mally!" or "Is this my wonderful grandbaby?"
You've texted me a lot this week during my work hours.	I know you're being your friendly, chatty self,	but it's been distracting and my boss talked to me about being on my phone too much.	I'll only be able to reply when I'm on my breaks from now on.
I'm not sure how to say this, but you compliment me on my dramatic weight loss each time you see me.	I know your intention is to be kind,	but I actually lost all this weight because my son just died, and I don't have any appetite anymore.	Please stop telling me that I "look so good now."
When you move everything around on my desk,	I know that you are trying to help me "be tidy,"	but now I can't find anything I need for this afternoon.	Will you wait until Fridays to "tidy up"? That would be much more helpful.
When you bring extra snacks for the soccer team only on the days I signed up to supply the snacks,	I think your intention is to be supportive and make sure there's lots of fresh options for everybody.	But I feel like not even making an effort to bring chips and cheese because you show up with fancy watermelon and grape shish kabobs.	Will you please stick to bringing snacks on the days you signed up for and let me do my snack days my own way?
When you invite me out to party,	I appreciate that you want to see me	but I think you forgot I am in recovery now.	Would you like to get coffee instead?
I know you are just asking a quick question	because you really care about your cats.	It's not good for my mental health to be "the veterinarian" on my days off.	Please call my office for an appointment if you want me to examine Isla and Igor for you.
When you ask me if I can still use scissors with my prosthetic hand,	I realize you're just being curious.	However, since how I use my hand is the only thing you ever ask me about, I'm starting to feel a little bit like the office sideshow.	I would appreciate it if you asked me about other things besides how my hand works.
You reminded me three times today that this will be my first Valentine's Day since coming out as a trans woman.	I get that you're excited for me,	but it's coming across as pressure instead of joy.	I would feel more supported if you would wait to talk about it until I bring it up first.

PRIVATE LATER SCRIPT: Remind, Acknowledge, Express, Ask

I locked the bathroom door, began to pull my leggings down, and glanced at the toilet seat.

Pee droplets. Again.

Eww.

This was the third time in a week that evidence my roommate had done his business right before me was left glistening on the seat.

I grabbed cleansing spray from the cupboard, wiped off the toilet seat, put the supplies back, washed my hands, and then pulled my leggings down to do what I had walked in there for.

Then I went down the hall to his room and knocked on the partially open door. "Cooper, do you have a minute to talk about an issue with the bathroom?"

Pausing his computer game and spinning toward me in his high-backed desk chair, he asked, "What's up, Kami?"

"There's been several days recently where I found pee dripped on the toilet seat. I've been cleaning it up each time, but I'd really rather not. Will you please be a bit more careful?"

Cooper blinked. "Uh, sure. Okay."

"Thanks! I appreciate it!" I stepped back into the hall. "Do you want this door closed?"

"It's fine like that."

"Okay! Enjoy your game!"

Was it awkward to ask my adult roommate to better monitor his bathroom habits? Yup! But I never saw pee on the seat again the rest of the year we shared a bathroom, so I think those few seconds of discomfort were absolutely worth it.

When I talked to Cooper, I used the Private Later Script, which has four parts:

Remind:

Describe what happened before that you are bringing up now.

There's been several days recently where I found pee dripped on the toilet seat.

Acknowledge:

Be upfront that you could've said something when it happened but you didn't.

I've been cleaning it up each time.

Express:

Say how you feel.

but I'd really rather not.

Ask:

Describe the behavior you want, the restitution you're seeking, or the boundary you are setting.

Will you please be a bit more careful?

The Private Later Script is a variation of the Private Now Script to be used in one-to-one conversations when you need to bring up an issue that has been happening for a while or has occurred in the past.

The challenge with bringing up an issue after days or weeks have passed is the other person usually doesn't remember it as well as you do. It's easier to recall events that have a lot of emotion attached.

When my classmate Henri told me at 10 years old, "You have a big nose when you smile," that was just a regular Tuesday to him. I've never forgotten it, and it took growing into my face during puberty to feel comfortable widely smiling around people again. If I saw Henri today and reminded him of what he had said over two decades ago, I know he wouldn't remember it at all.

So, how long can you wait before you can no longer use the Private Later Script with someone?

When this has come up in my boundary coaching sessions, I always turn it around and ask, "What is the goal? What do you hope to achieve by reminding this person what happened and how you feel about it?"

Sometimes the answer is, "I want closure. I want the chance to tell them how I feel about what they did."

I believe closure is a gift only we can give ourselves. You are the expert on your specific situation, and if telling that person how you feel about something that happened months, years, or decades later is what you need to do, it's okay to choose that.

Personally, my limit is four to six weeks of bringing up a past issue. If it's an ongoing pattern that's been happening for more than six weeks and I haven't spoken up yet, then I have to reevaluate if it's really a big enough deal to say something at all.

If it's been longer than a month or so, before I decide to talk to the person I use the Reply Letter Technique.

First, I write them a letter (one I'll *never* send) listing all the feelings I'm having. I vent it all out. Even if it's harsh or ugly or cruel, I put it all on paper. Next I get a new page and write a letter to myself pretending to be them replying to my first letter. I include the apology I'm seeking, the empathy I want, and whatever needs to be said, so I can have closure. Then I read both letters out loud in private. There's usually tears at this point. Finally, I burn both letters.

Out of the 15 times I've personally used the Reply Letter Technique, there have only been two people that I decided to talk to in person about my feelings on choices they had made in the past.

With one of those people, I got amazing closure and I'm so grateful I did it. It had been over three months since things happened, and while the conversation was intense, it was incredibly cathartic.

The other time? Not good. He said, "That didn't happen. That doesn't sound like me. I don't remember that." I pushed back with, "I remember it." But he just wouldn't accept it. It was a new type of pain trying to convince someone who hurt me that they actually did hurt me.

So if you're looking for closure, I highly recommend trying the Reply Letter Technique first. Then if after destroying the letters, you still want to go ahead with the Private Later Script after months, years, or decades, know that you have my blessing!

The other common answer to the question about what a client's goal in reminding someone about something that happened in the past is, "I want them to change. I want them to never do it again!"

I think it is really admirable that you want to make the world a better place, prevent harm, and let people know that the impact of their choices had long reaching effects. If you're trying to decide whether or not to use the Private Later Script with someone after a long time because you want them to make different choices in the future, I invite you to consider what your relationship with that person is like:

1. Is this someone that you interact with on a regular basis?
2. Is there a large reservoir of trust between you?
3. Are they in a position of power over vulnerable individuals?
4. Do you think they'll be receptive to your unsolicited feedback?

If you can answer yes to one or more of those four questions, then it will probably go well. If the only yes is to their position of power over vulnerable individuals, it's important to try anyway, but since you're telling them bummer news they didn't ask for, it might be a fiasco.

If you can't say yes to any of those four questions, I caution you that your efforts to change someone else who isn't asking you to help them change are probably not going to work out.

Especially because the longer it's been since whatever happened occurred or the longer it's been of that behavior repeating, the less likely they are to perceive it the same way as you. What's a big deal to you is most likely a small thing to them.

Again, you are the expert on your own situation. Do what you feel is best.

Now that we've discussed when to use the Private Later Script, let's go over what the script includes. As I said, it's a variation of the Private Now Script so you'll notice several similarities.

Each part of the script can be mixed and matched with the other parts, like you can swap most Acknowledges for any other and it still works.

THE REMIND

Remind them what the words or actions were that you're referring to.

Be as specific as possible. Instead of, "The other day when you said that thing to me," try "When we were talking on Tuesday and you mentioned that you don't like me borrowing your clothes because I stretch your sweaters out . . ."

This part is like the Private Now Script where you defined the not-okay behavior. Except instead of describing what's happening right now, you're recalling something that happened hours, days, or possibly weeks ago.

THE ACKNOWLEDGE

Acknowledge that you didn't say something before because you weren't sure what to say.

One of my sisters—who is one of my absolute favorite people on the planet—needs a lot more time than I do to figure out how she's feeling when something not okay happens between us. She needs even more time to decide what she wants to do about it.

There was a season of our relationship where it would really stress me out and hurt my feelings that she would bring up stuff that happened like two weeks previously. It had been a big deal to her, but I could barely remember it because it wasn't even a blip on my radar!

Her willingness to acknowledge and take accountability for not saying something at the time the issue occurred and explain *why* she was bringing it up so much later really smoothed everything over.

Now I understand how her need to process her emotions is different from mine. I had assumed when she waited weeks to tell me something wasn't okay that she spent all that time raging like a bonfire! Turns out it's more like a soup on the back burner of a stove that just simmers quietly until it's ready.

I trust her to tell me within a few weeks if there's a problem between us on her side. She trusts that I'll tell her right away, and if I haven't said anything, then everything is good!

Even with this high level of comfort around saying the thing to each other, it's still really helpful for me when she acknowledges, "I didn't say anything last week because I needed time to process."

If you're a slower emotional processor like my sister, I highly encourage you to memorize some Acknowledge phrases because it will make boundary setting much smoother.

Here are 10 examples pulled from the table at the end of this chapter:

1. I didn't say anything then, but I wanted to tell you now.
2. I was kind of in shock, so I didn't speak up at the moment.
3. I didn't say anything at the time because I didn't know what to say, but I wanted to let you know . . .
4. I dropped the ball on this.
5. This is the last time I'm going to say it.
6. I haven't reached out until now.

7. I let it go then, but I can't stop thinking about it.

8. I know I left you on read; I needed some time to figure out how I wanted to respond.

9. I waited a few weeks to be sure before I said anything.

10. I'm telling you now that . . .

THE EXPRESS

Here is the part where you use "I feel" statements to describe how you're feeling about what happened. It is similar to the third part of the Private Now Script where you explain the impact their words or actions have had. Use descriptive emotion words. Do you feel uncomfortable, sad, frustrated, nervous, overwhelmed, shocked, disappointed, annoyed, etc.? Express to them how you're feeling.

Reasonable and kind people will care that their actions or words created distress for you. If I'm talking to my best friend, I will use more detailed emotional language like, "I felt really scared and sad. I felt like I was the only kid in class not invited to the birthday party." If I'm talking to a business contact, I will use more staid language like, "Candidly, I found it quite upsetting." or "It's not an experience I'm looking to repeat."

If you're not sure how much is appropriate to share in certain settings, pick only one emotion word to start with. "I felt stressed about the last-minute notice" or "I felt worried that things aren't okay between us." This part can be as long or as brief as you need to communicate how you feel.

THE ASK

The Ask is when you describe what you want to have happen in the future. It is similar to the fourth part of the Private Now Script, where you describe the behavior you'd like to see moving forward. This can also be asking for a specific type of restitution or setting a boundary.

The more direct you are in what you ask for, the easier it will be for people to say yes or no to it. Especially since you're coming back later after you've had time to think about everything, it's extra important to figure out what you want from the other person. Do you want an apology? Do you want repayment? Do you want them to explain why they did what they did? Do you want them to change something? What exactly do you want? Be prepared to ask for it.

PUTTING THE PRIVATE LATER SCRIPT TOGETHER

If you need a script to go back to someone and say something, I encourage you to write out what you want to say first using the Remind, Acknowledge, Express, Ask formula. Here are 10 examples to get you started:

Remind	Acknowledge	Express	Ask
The last time we visited you, you told Ramni if he gave you a hug that you'd give him a piece of candy.	I didn't say anything then, but I wanted to tell you now	that I'm teaching Ramni that he's the boss of his body. He's learning that he doesn't owe anyone, even his favorite auntie, a hug.	Please just ask Ramni he wants hugs from no on instead of bribing h with candy.
Last week after game night, you said you like when I come to play because, "every group needs a loser."	I was kind of in shock so I didn't speak up at the moment,	but it really hurt my feelings! I know you were joking, but it isn't funny to me.	I'd appreciate it if you didn't say that again.
Last night when we were fooling around in bed you said my penis is "fun sized."	I didn't say anything at the time because I didn't know what to say, but I wanted to let you know	that comment killed the mood for me.	Please don't say that again.
We talked last month about doing some collaborative Instagram posts together.	I dropped the ball on planning this	and I'm feeling a little overwhelmed.	Is that still something y want to do? If so, will you take over planning what we're going to do
I've told you before that "jokes" about me having pancake boobs when I wear my binder aren't okay.	This is the last time I'm going to say it.	I feel uncomfortable with how much you want to talk about my chest shape every time you see me.	Can you please stop?
I loaned you $900 at the beginning of the pandemic, and I told you to pay it back when you could.	I haven't reached out until now	but I feel like two years is a lot longer than I had planned to have a debt between us.	When do you think you be sending me that money?
Leaving the restaurant on Sunday, you didn't tip the server on our check.	I let it go then, but I can't stop thinking about it.	I feel shocked you wouldn't tip even 15 percent but especially because they went out of their way to accommodate our large group. I'm not okay dining out without tipping where it's standard.	Will you explain what happened? Did you lea a cash tip I didn't see?
You texted me yesterday that you're only interested in going out again if I promise to have sex with you afterward.	I know I left you on read; I needed some time to figure out how I wanted to respond.	I feel really disappointed that you said you're okay with my demisexuality and that it takes me a while to want to sleep with someone. But now it's been two dates, and you're pushing me for something I'm not interested in.	Please delete my numb
A couple weeks ago we talked about getting a second dog to keep Oscar company. You promised me you'd play fetch with him when you get home from school every day to show you're ready for another pet.	I waited a few weeks to be sure, but I've only seen you in the backyard once since that conversation.	I feel disappointed.	Do you want to try ago or should we decide Oscar is enough dog fo this family for now?
Our annual expo is in two months, and last year I got the impression you wanted everyone on the team to eat every meal together all three days.	I'm telling you now	that it was really stressful for me to not have any downtime to myself.	Can we make a new p this year where we pick one team meal each da instead of three?

PART III

BOUNDARY PHRASES ALPHABETICAL BY CATEGORY

How to Use
Boundary Phrases

My sister is considered a tall woman at six feet one inch in height. All her life people have jokingly asked her, "How's the weather up there?"

When we were kids, we decided the best answer was for her to say, "It's raining!" and spit on their heads! To my knowledge, she never actually did this, but it was good to have a pre-planned response to a frequent question.

This part of the book is just that: pre-planned responses to frequent questions or statements that you keep getting on specific topics.

We all have something about us that could be considered "different." If you have a limb difference, strangers might ask, "What happened to your leg?" If you're a Black woman with textured hair, coworkers may ask, "Can I touch your hair?" If you have a cluttered house, your mother-in-law could say, "It's pretty messy in here, isn't it?"

In the following chapters you'll find thousands of boundary phrase suggestions to memorize so you'll be prepared to say the thing!

ADHD & Autism

In hindsight, I'm shocked it took me until I was 32 years old to realize that I am autistic. By that point, I had one autistic sibling and four autistic close friends, I'd dated several autistic people, and I had spent the last year reading online about autism and following dozens of autistic content creators on social media.

Yet when I was told by a lovely autistic man I'd been flirting with on a dating app, "You have kind of an autistic vibe. Have you ever looked into that?" I was shocked! My love and admiration for autistic people prevented me in a roundabout way from realizing I am also autistic. I saw amazing traits, like pattern recognition, direct communication, intense empathy, passion for niche interests, fierce commitment to justice, etc. and didn't realize that's me too. But once I could see it, I couldn't unsee it.

My favorite part of that story is how many of my other friends also soon realized they are neurodivergent after my diagnosis. We really do find each other! Many of my loved ones are both autistic and ADHD. I'm actually rare in my circles being only autistic without ADHD, but in my experience, most neurodivergent people tend to think alike, so it all works out great!

Note that I don't use the term *neurodivergent* when referring to only ADHD and autistic people. It's my understanding that neurodivergence includes other conditions such as Tourette's, dyspraxia, dyscalculia, dyslexia, traumatic brain injuries, and (depending on who you ask) PTSD, CPTSD, depression, anxiety, obsessive disorders, and more. ADHD and autism are just two colors of the neurodivergent rainbow and are the focus of this section.

Here are several statements and a scenario, with lists of possible responses, to help you know what to say when people comment about ADHD and autism.

ADHD

"Just try harder!"

- The issue isn't the lack of effort. The issue is I have an executive functioning condition that makes certain tasks incredibly difficult. It's part of my disability.

- If the issue was the amount of effort I'm exerting, this would be done by now. This isn't a "try harder" situation.

- When you do it, it's like you're lifting a 5-pound weight. When I do it, it's a 50-pound weight. Saying, "try harder" because you think I am struggling with a 5-pound weight is not helpful. What we are lifting isn't the same.

- I know when you say, "just try harder," your intention is to be helpful and supportive. It comes across as "what's wrong with you that you aren't making an effort." A better option would be, "What can I do to support you?" or "I believe in your ability to figure this out, and I'm here if you need me."

"Why don't you just get a planner/make a list/write it on the calendar?"

- Our brains work differently. I'm glad that making a list is a tool that helps you. I've tried it, and that's not a tool that helps me.

- I get that your intention is to be helpful. When you phrase it like "why don't you just," it comes across like "What's wrong with you that you haven't thought of this simple solution to your problem?" I know that's not what you meant. A better option would be asking, "What strategies have you found to help you stay organized?"

- I appreciate that you want to help me figure this out. I get that my process doesn't make sense to you, but I am doing it in a way that works for me.

- I know you're trying to be helpful, but I am not in the place for suggestions on how I can do this differently. Please wait until I ask you for organizing ideas before offering them.

"Stop being so lazy."

- Are you trying to start a conversation about the overwhelming amount of things on my plate right now? Because that is not the right way to go about it. A better option is asking, "It looks like you have a lot going on. Do you want to talk about that?"

- What you call "lazy," I call "doing the very best I can with the resources and support I have."

- That's not a kind or helpful thing to say. Please don't make comments like that to me again.

"Just wait a minute! Be patient."

- I think you're assuming my excitement is impatience. I'm not upset; I'm really looking forward to this!

- It's okay if you need more time. You're always welcome to ask for that. It's not okay to shame me for being excited.

- Do you need more time? I'm happy to go find something else to do until you're ready.

- When you say "a minute," to me that means anywhere from 60 seconds to 20 minutes. I'm okay to wait that long if that's what you need. If it's more than 20 minutes, please let me know.

"What is the matter with you? Why are you making it harder on yourself?"

- That's not a helpful or kind line of questioning. If you're trying to be supportive, a better option is saying, "I don't understand what's happening, but I'd really like to. Can we talk about this?"

- My brain works differently than yours. I'm not deliberately "making it harder" on myself.

- Are you trying to start a conversation about how my disability works? Because that is not the right way to go about it.

- I'm not sure what your intention is, but what you just said came across in a really shaming "there's something wrong with you and I don't approve of your choices" type of way. That doesn't encourage me to share with you what's going on or reach out to you if I need help.

"You would think a grown adult would know where their important ID is! Why do you lose stuff all the time?"

- My disability impacts my working memory and organization. That means my brain's ability to keep track of key information is different from that of non-ADHD people.

- My executive functioning is not related to my age, and it's not helpful to say it is. Please don't make shaming comments like that.

- I understand that you're frustrated that we can't find my ID right now. I am too. But it's not okay to shame me for accidentally losing my ID. Let's take a break from looking and try again after lunch.

- When you say stuff like, "A grown adult should know where their ID is!" it comes across like, "You're an incompetent child, and I think less of you because you accidentally lost your wallet again." I get that losing stuff isn't something you've ever struggled with, so it feels ridiculous to you that it happens to me so much, but your shaming comments aren't going to make me stop losing things. It will make me stop telling you about it. Is that your goal?

"Aren't you supposed to grow out of that? Only kids have ADHD."

- Nope! ADHD is a lifelong condition. Sometimes it looks like people grow out of it because they've developed strategies to make it easier to live with, but adults continue to have ADHD.

- Sounds like I'm the first adult ADHDer you know! That's awesome! ADHD is a lifelong condition and not something I'll ever "grow out of."

"Stop playing on your phone when I'm talking to you!"

- My brain works differently than yours, and it's easier for me to listen to you when I've also got this game going. I could switch to a fidget toy or doodling on paper instead, but I need to be doing something to be able to focus on what you're saying.

- I know it looks like I'm not listening if you didn't know I'm ADHD, but this is how I listen best. You've got my attention; please keep going with what you were saying.

"We're all a little ADHD sometimes."

- In what way are you ADHD? Have you ever been evaluated?

- Maybe some of the behaviors are common, but the frequency is not. For example, everyone gets thirsty, but if you're drinking a full glass every 15 minutes, you probably should get checked out.

"ADHD is just made up to get drugs."

- That is both inaccurate and offensive. Please don't say things like that around me.

- If you're trying to start a debate about the validity of my diagnosis, it's not working. I'm not discussing this with you.

AUTISM

"He is low-functioning autistic."

- Is that the language he uses to refer to himself? I personally don't use functioning labels, but if that's what he uses, I want to respect that.

- It's my understanding that the idea of "high-functioning" or "low-functioning" autism was created by allistic (non-autistic) people to identify how obviously inconvenient a particular autistic person is. Autism is autism, even when support needs vary.

- I've often heard that phrase used to describe someone with intellectual or developmental disabilities, as well as autism. Is that what you meant?

- Why is the level of support he needs relevant to this conversation?

"You're supposed to say 'person with autism.'"

- Most autistic adults prefer identity-first language.

- The phrase "person with autism" puts the person first, while the phrase "autistic person" puts their identity first. As an autistic person, I use identity-first language.

- I appreciate your advocacy! However, most autistic adults prefer identity-first language, so that's what I'm going to use unless an individual autistic adult asks me to use person-first language for them.

- The other day you interrupted me when I referred to myself as an "autistic person" to say I should use "person with autism" instead. I didn't say anything at that time because I needed to gather my thoughts, but I want you to know it's really not okay to correct how an autistic person refers to themself. It's like if you said, "Call me Dave" and I said, "No, your name is David." You're the expert on your own name, and I'm the expert on my own autistic identity.

"It's Asperger's, not autism."

- We're actually right in the middle of society changing how we refer to autism. Asperger's used to be a standalone diagnosis, but this changed in 2013. Now it's categorized under the Autism Spectrum Disorder.

- I support you in using whatever term you want to refer to yourself. That's your right. I personally do not use the word *Asperger's* to refer to autistic people.

- May I share something with you that it sounds like you may not know? The majority of the autistic community no longer use the Asperger's label, because it has been alleged that Hans Asperger was a doctor who recommended autistic children for euthanasia by the Nazis in the 20th century. That's where the term *Asperger's Syndrome* comes from. You'll probably meet individuals who use that label for themselves, and it is okay to respect their choice, but generally *Asperger's* is not considered the right term anymore.

"Everyone's a little bit autistic!"

- No. Autism is a genetic neurotype. I can send you more information if you're interested, but I won't debate this with you.

- Well, autism is genetic, so it's common for people to believe that because they themselves are autistic, so is their whole family!

- May I offer you some feedback about what you just said? [They consent to receive feedback.] It's common for people to believe that "everyone's a little bit autistic" because they see autistic traits as normal from their own childhood because their family is autistic. So while it's not true that "everyone's a little bit autistic," it might be true that you or your family are autistic.

"You're very rude." or "That's a rude question to ask."

- I'm autistic and sometimes when I ask questions to help me understand what someone is saying, it comes across as rude. I'm sorry that happened in this case. I hope we can continue on with what you were saying because I really want to know the point you were making.

- I understand that what I said felt rude to you, but I don't understand why it felt rude. Will you explain further so I can avoid making that mistake again?

- Oh! I'm sorry. I am a curious person for sure, and I can absolutely come across as rude when my enthusiasm gets the better of me and I ask overly personal questions. My apologies!

"You need to go out more and talk to people. Stop hiding in your room so much!"

- The boiling water softens the potato but hardens the egg. Not everyone reacts the same way in the same conditions. Personally, being around a lot of people can make me feel like I'm being boiled!

- I get that being out socializing and meeting new people makes you happy! Personally, I am much happier with a lot of alone time and a select friend group. We're wired differently, and that's okay.

- Are you trying to start a conversation about your concerns that I don't have enough friends and you're worried that I'm lonely? Because a better way would be asking, "Can we talk about how you're feeling lately? I've noticed you've been spending a lot of time in your room, and I wanted to check in to see if you're okay."

- I appreciate your concern, but I'm happy with the amount of socializing I'm doing. And I love being in my room; it's my favorite place!

"Stop flapping your hands! You look like a dang bird!"

- I'm stimming (a repetetive motion or vocalization sometimes used by neurodivergent people to calm themselves in times of stress) to regulate my nervous system because I'm trying to avoid a sensory meltdown. If it bothers you, you don't have to watch.

- Hand flapping is a really common stimming behavior for autistic people to release excess emotions. You're welcome to join me; you might enjoy it!

- Stimming is like taking the lid off a boiling pot. It stops it from spilling over until you can turn down the heat. I'm really overwhelmed right now, and your yelling is making it worse. I need to stim, or I need to leave.

- I'm not going to stop helping myself in a way that doesn't hurt anyone just because you think it looks weird. It's okay for me to stim!

"You're too pretty to be autistic!"

- I hope you didn't mean it this way, but you just said, "I think autistic people are ugly." You can compliment me without bashing my community.

- Part of me is curious about what you meant by that, but most of me wants to just ignore that unfortunate comment and move on, so that's what I'm going to do.

- What you just said came across like, "I believe I can identify disabled people based on how attractive they are to me," which is both ignorant and insulting. Please don't ever say that again.

"He's probably autistic. He doesn't understand social rules."

- If he's autistic, the best option is to be really clear about what the expectations are instead of giving out hints he's not getting. If he's not autistic, the best option is to be really clear about what the expectations are instead of giving out hints he's not getting. Either way, you need to be clear and direct.

- What did he say when you told him it wasn't okay to bring his friend to your party without checking with you first? Did you directly say that to him? How is he supposed to know it's not okay if you didn't tell him?

- I've had the opposite experience with autistic people! They are often dedicated students of social rules because they are aware it's a potential weakness. They often work extra hard to know what's okay and not okay to say and do.

- Does his misunderstanding of social rules only play out in his favor, or does it happen no matter the setting? Because if his behavior affects everyone all the time, then I'd agree it might be autism, and someone needs to tell him what is okay and what's not. But if it's only in his favor, that's just jerk behavior, and he needs to be asked to stop. We don't need to excuse it by assigning him a diagnosis we aren't qualified to give.

NON-VOCAL

You're a bystander seeing someone who is non-vocal being ignored by a customer service worker. They are using AAC (augmentative and alternative communication, typically a symbol board, cell phone, tablet, or pen and paper).

To the person being ignored, you can say:

- He's obviously ignoring you. Would you like me to say something?

- It's not okay that they're ignoring you. May I get a manager for you?

- You were totally clear, and she's being ridiculous to insist you speak when it's obvious what you're asking for. May I help you?

To the person doing the ignoring, you can say:

- Hey! Don't ignore them. That's really not okay.

- Whoa. They're obviously communicating clearly, and you're insisting they be verbal right now. That's not cool.

- You don't know why someone might be non-vocal. It's really ableist to insist they communicate the way *you* think they should.

Animals

Animals—both wild and domestic—are a big part of our lives! This creates many opportunities for triangulated boundaries. That means there are three parties involved: you, me, and the animal.

For example, I may need you to stop your dog, Buddy, from jumping on me. I'm interacting with both you and your dog. Depending on whether I'm a friend or a stranger, you might be okay with me preventing Buddy from leaping onto my lap, or you might prefer to corral his excitement yourself.

If I express that I dislike Buddy, who is a cherished member of your family, you might think less of me. But what if I'm afraid of being around Buddy because of bad past experiences with dogs? Do you pick Buddy over me, vice versa, or find a way to accommodate us both? Boundary setting when animals are involved can get complicated!

Here are 20 statements and scenarios I've come across about animals, each with a list of potential responses, to help you navigate these triangulated relationships.

PETS

"It's okay. He's friendly! He just likes to enthusiastically say hello to everybody!"

- I'm glad he's friendly, but please don't let him jump on me.

- He definitely looks friendly! I'm not okay with being jumped on, but I'd love to pet him if you hold him first.

- Whoa. I'm actually not comfortable around dogs, so if you would grab him, I'd really appreciate it!

- I wish I could say hi back, but with my allergies, it would leave me sneezing all day, so please keep him from touching me.

"Oh, she would never bite anyone. She's just play-fighting!"

- I'm not familiar enough with dog body language to tell the difference between play fighting and real fighting, so I'd be more comfortable if you kept her over there with you.

- I'm so glad she'd never bite anyone, but I'd rather not risk it. Will you distract her so she stops focusing on me? Thank you!

Their off-leash dog aggressively runs up to your leashed dog. The owner is just watching and not intervening.

- Hey! I need to keep my dog away from other dogs, so please come get yours!

- Please grab your dog to give me time to move mine away.

- I wanted to talk to you about your dog running up to my dog when we pass your yard on our walks. So far it results in both dogs getting upset and barking at each other. If there was another option to leave the neighborhood without going past your house and disturbing your dog, I would, but this is the only route to the park. Is there something we could do to make this easier on everybody?

Your neighbor's dog is barking for hours when they are gone.

- Hey, I'm not sure if you're aware, but your dog has been barking a lot when she's home alone. And by a lot, I mean yesterday she barked for over three hours and seemed really distressed.

- I apologize for disturbing you so late, but your dog has been barking for over an hour, and I wanted to make sure everything was okay.

Their cat scratches you, snags your sweater, or ruins your stuff.

- Oops! He scratched me! Will you put him in the other room until I leave? Thanks!

- I know cats will be cats, but last time I was here, Moxie snagged the bottom of my sweater and ruined it. What can we do to avoid that from happening again?

- I need to talk to you about something serious. Is now a good time? [They say yes, or you find another time to discuss it.] Sometime today while we were gone, Pawbrey went into my room and peed on my bed. This has never happened before. I don't know why it happened now, and I'm really upset about it. Will you please pay for a replacement pillow and to get my comforter professionally cleaned? I will make sure my door is always closed when I'm not home from now on.

"I hate cats. They're so stuck-up and mean!"

- Cats have boundaries! If they don't want to be touched, they don't allow it. I really admire that trait!

- Cats are very different from dogs. You can't read their body language in the same way.

- It's okay if you don't like cats, but it's not okay if you are unkind to cats. As long as you let them have space to do their thing, it's all good!

"Wow! You really are a crazy cat lady! That's a lot of cats!"

- I think it's all relative. Some people think that having any cats is "a lot."

- I love you saying that as a joke, but I don't like being called a "crazy cat lady." Please don't say that again.

- I don't like that term; it feels sexist to me. If a man had five cats, he wouldn't be called a "crazy cat gentleman."

They hit/push/kick your pet.

- Hey! Don't touch my pet! That's really not okay!

- If my pet is in your way, please ask me to move her instead of pushing her. She's a lot smaller than you and could get hurt!

- Nope! That's animal abuse. I'm reporting this immediately.

They try to feed your pet human-food without checking with you first.

- Wait! She can't eat human-food; it hurts her stomach. I have a treat you can give her if you want to.

- Thank you for wanting to share your food with them. That's not something they can safely eat. Please check with me before trying to feed them anything.

- I get that you want to give him a bite of what you're enjoying. However he is on a strict diet for health reasons and can't eat that.

SERVICE ANIMALS

A stranger tries to pet your service animal while she is working.

- Please don't distract my service animal while she's working.

- Please don't touch her while she's wearing her service vest. Later when she is on break and we take the vest off, then you can pet her.

- Oh! I know it's hard to resist petting such a cute face, but please check with me before touching them while they're working.

"Why do you need a service animal?"

- I have a personal rule that I don't discuss my medical conditions when I'm out having fun; it tends to put a damper on the party.

- I get that you're just curious and don't mean any harm, but that's a really intrusive question to ask a stranger, and it's not one I'm going to answer.

- If you're trying to start a conversation about my service animal, a better question is, "What's her name?"

- Your curiosity doesn't entitle you to my private medical information.

"You can't bring that animal in here! No pets allowed!"

- She's not a pet; she's a trained service animal I need for my disability.

- I'm disabled and need my service animal with me for my medical safety.

"Pit bulls can't be service dogs! Only Labradors or German shepherds."

- That's a common misconception. As long as the dog has the right temperament, any breed can be a service dog.

- Are you trying to start a conversation about service dog breeds, or are you accusing me of having a fake service dog? Because I'm sure hoping it's the first one!

"I'm not going to let you bring that dog in here unless you can prove she's really a service animal. Is she registered with the ADA?"

- It sounds like you're not familiar with the ADA regulations for service animals. It's not legal to ask me to prove she's a service dog or for any type of registration. I can, however, tell you that she is required because of my disability and share what work she is trained to perform.

- The ADA doesn't register service animals, but it does regulate what a business owner can ask about service animals. What you just said is not allowed. You can find the official rules and regulations listed on the Americans with Disabilities Act (ADA) website. Will you please allow me access with my dog now? Thank you.

- There are a lot of common misunderstandings about service animals, and I didn't know anything about them until I started the process to get my dog. Would you like me to send you a link to the ADA website that explains everything you need to know about service animals as a business owner?

WILD ANIMALS

"Look at this turtle I caught! I'm gonna take him home with me!"

- I love that you're so excited about the turtle, but it's not okay to capture wild animals to keep as pets. It's bad for the local population and is actually illegal in some places. Can we take a photo or video of you with the turtle instead, and then let him go?

- I'm going to say this as kindly as I possibly can: If you were already someone who was successfully keeping turtles at home, you'd know that taking a wild one out of its natural environment is not okay. And since you don't already know that, that tells me you don't currently have a turtle paludarium at home. Please let the turtle go. If you take it home without knowing what you're doing, it's probably going to be unhappy or die.

They deliberately swerve to try to hit an animal with their car.

- Wow. What you just did to that animal was wrong and immediately changed how I see you as a person! I need to leave now because I can't be around you anymore.

- Deliberately hurting something smaller than you just because you can is the definition of cruelty. That's really messed up, and I'm shocked you would treat an innocent animal like that!

They are feeding human-food to a wild animal.

- Oh no! I know you're trying to do a good thing and feed him, but that trains the animal to approach humans for food and will get him hurt or get people hurt. Please don't do that.

- May I offer you some information it seems like you may not know? [They consent to receiving information.] I know it's fun to feed the ducks, but bread is unfortunately not a good choice. It doesn't have the nutrients a duck needs, but they get filled up so then they don't eat other things and can become sick. Better options are mealworms, birdseed, spinach, or kale.

They are trying to pet a wild animal or to take a close-up photo.

- Hold up! As fluffy as she is, she's wild and will hurt you if you get too close.

- That's not safe! I know he looks calm now, but that can change in an instant, so please back away slowly without making eye contact.

"I kill every bee I see because I want to get them before they get me!"

- Bees are valuable pollinators. Without them, humans will probably stop existing. Please don't kill bees.

- My understanding is that seeking out and attacking bees is more likely to get you stung versus giving them a wide berth.

- I think it's one thing if the bees are in your home and you need to get them out, but it's another thing if you are in their home outside and killing bees out of spite. That's a pretty unfortunate attitude because bees are precious pollinators.

- I'm not okay with you killing bees around me. Your choices are to leave the bees alone or we can only hang out inside where there are no bees.

Anxiety & Depression

The first time my therapist suggested medication for my persistent depressive disorder, I said no. Absolutely not!

I didn't grow up in a family that used medicine. The first time I ever took an ibuprofen pain reliever, I was 23 years old. Before that moment, I didn't know that pain meds were so helpful. It blew my mind!

At this point, the idea of going on a daily dose of mental health meds was completely outside my comfort zone.

I did weekly therapy for a year. I got a lot better in some ways, but I still struggled to get out of bed in the morning and connect with people, and I had no energy for hobbies or interests, and felt like the sad donkey Eeyore from *Winnie the Pooh* all the time.

When my therapist brought up medication again, this time I said yes. I got my prescription and nervously started taking it. The pharmacist told me it would take two or three weeks to notice anything. Two weeks went by . . . nothing. Three weeks went by . . . still exactly the same. Three weeks and three days . . . the lights came on!

While medication might not be the best choice for everyone, and it should be thoroughly discussed with your doctor, it was a great choice for me and greatly improved my life. The experience has made me much more open and understanding of mental health journeys of all kinds.

If you have anxiety or depression, I hope you can get the support you need for the lights to come on for you too. Here are several statements and suggested responses about anxiety, social anxiety, and depression to help you out.

ANXIETY

"You're overreacting."

- Yes. That is exactly what an anxiety disorder is. I have an overactive amygdala that can't tell the difference between a mountain and a molehill. Everything feels like a mountain all the time. Thankfully I'm getting the support I need to help manage my symptoms, but today I'm having a hard time, and telling me that I'm "overreacting" is making it worse. Please give me some space.

- I know that what my anxiety disorder chooses to see as a threat isn't logical. It's my brain doing its best to keep me alive. Please don't tell me I'm "overreacting." A more helpful option is, "That seems really scary for you. Will you tell me what you're thinking?"

"Everyone has anxiety." or "Everyone gets anxious sometimes."

- You're right that humans experience moments of anxiety. That's different from having an anxiety disorder. It's like comparing a chihuahua and a Tyrannosaurus rex. Sure, they both bite. But one has much bigger teeth!

- Are you trying to start a conversation about how mental health disorders differ from general emotional responses? Because that's not the best way to go about it. You could ask, "I want to understand what makes an anxiety disorder different from how everyone gets anxious sometimes. Will you explain it to me?"

"Just stop worrying about it!" "Just relax!" "Chill out!" "Snap out of it!"

- I get that you're frustrated with my anxiety. I am too. It's okay if you need to take a break from talking about this, but it's not okay to snap at me for having a mental health disorder.

- If your goal is to help me feel better, telling me to "chill out" is having the opposite effect. What would be helpful is if you give me a few minutes to compose myself. Excuse me. [walk away]

"It's all in your head."

- Yes. Anxiety is a mental health disorder. It is very much in my head.

- I know you're saying that to be helpful because you care about me, and I appreciate that. It's having the opposite effect because it sounds like, "You aren't perceiving reality accurately," which is really scary. A better option would be, "Let's sort through this together. What's on your mind?"

"You're being ridiculous. Nothing bad is going to happen."

- Shaming me for having ancestors who were the most watchful members of the group so we all could survive to the present day is not helpful! I'm literally wired to anticipate all potential bad things. It's how my brain works!

- I know you don't get it, but I need you to either respect how I feel right now or leave me alone while I gather my thoughts.

"It's not as bad as you think."

- I know you're trying to be helpful, and I appreciate that. A more helpful thing to say right now would be, "I care about you, and I want to support you. Would you like a glass of water and a few minutes to yourself?"

- When you say that, my first thought is, "You're right. It's worse." And it escalates my mental spiral. Will you stick to, "Take your time. I'm here for as long as you need."? Thanks.

"You're just exaggerating for attention!"

- Anyone who has to exaggerate their symptoms to get their needs met isn't being listened to or supported very well. That's sad for them, and I'm grateful you would never do that to me. If anything, I'm downplaying how bad it is because I need help, but I don't want you to feel sorry for me. Will you please listen to me tell you about what's going on?

- Humans do need attention! You don't have to believe me about my experience and you can decide you don't want to help me, but it's not okay to try to shame me for attempting to get my human need for attention met.

"You have no idea what it means to be truly mentally ill."

- This isn't a competition of who has the worst condition. Your mental illness can be really hard for you and my mental illness can be really hard for me, and there's no need to minimize what someone else is going through.

- When you say that, what I hear is, "I was taught that my experience isn't valid, so now I invalidate others' experiences because I'm projecting my own anger onto them." That is really sad, and I hope you get the support you need to work through that.

SOCIAL ANXIETY

"Calm down. They aren't going to bite you!"

- When in the history of humankind has loudly barking at someone to "calm down" ever helped anyone relax, take a deep breath, and center themselves? That's not helpful. Please don't say that to me.

- Minimizing my anxiety is giving me additional anxiety about you being upset with me for having anxiety in the first place! What I need is a few minutes to gather my thoughts. Excuse me.

"They're not going to care."

- They might not care, but *I care*—and that's the focus at this moment. What I need from you is to hold my hand and tell me that even if they say I'm the worst ever or laugh me out of the room, you'll still love me and support me and we'll go get ice cream afterward.

- My social anxiety isn't really about them and how they feel. It's about my overactive brain anticipating potential threats to try to keep me safe and alive! It's more helpful if you promise to step in and make conversation if I give you the signal so I can take a moment to breathe.

DEPRESSION

"Your life is good. You have nothing to be depressed about!"

- Depression is a mood disorder with lots of potential factors. Life being "good" or not is just one of them. It also comes from genetics, stress, medications, brain chemistry, and more. Telling me I "have nothing to be depressed about" isn't helpful.

- If you're trying to start a conversation about my mental health, this isn't the best way to go about it. A better option would be asking, "I don't understand depression as well as I'd like to. Can we talk about how you've been feeling lately so I can better support you?"

"Just be happy! Isn't there anything you're grateful for?"

- I am grateful for a lot in my life, and I also have a depressive mood disorder. One doesn't cancel out the other.

- I think I have every right to feel a wide range of emotions. I'm not going to pretend to be happy to help you feel comfortable.

"Have you tried yoga?" "You just need more sunshine." "I've heard kale can help with depression!"

- I understand your intention is to be helpful, but please don't offer suggestions for my mental health unless I directly ask you to.

- I appreciate that you care about me so much that you want to solve my depressive disorder. If love was the answer, I'd be symptom-free because of how much you love me. Unfortunately that's not how it works, and suggestions like, "Have you tried getting more sunshine?" aren't helpful. Please hold off on any ideas unless I specifically ask you for them. Thanks!

"Everyone gets depressed sometimes."

- When you say "everyone," do you actually mean "everyone," or are you referring to yourself? Do you feel intense sadness, low energy, and an overwhelming sense of doom all the time? Because that's depression.

- There's a difference between having a bad day and having months or years of a dark cloud hanging over you. I know you're saying that to try to help, but a more helpful option would be, "I believe that how you feel is real. That's really tough. Do you want to talk about it or be distracted from it right now?"

"Men don't get depression."

- You're right that cis women are more likely to be diagnosed with depression, but there's also research showing that cis men are less likely than cis women to seek out the support needed to get a diagnosis. It's a hot mess all around, and I think what really matters is I'm depressed and I wanted to talk to you about it. Is that something you have the space for right now?

- All genders can have depression. What you just said is a myth that hurts everybody by reinforcing gender stereotypes about what it means to "be a man." Please don't repeat that around me again.

"Don't be weak."

- Expressing my vulnerable feelings and telling you that I'm struggling with my mental health is the opposite of weak. How dare you shame me for trying to get some support! That's really messed up! I really expected better from you, which is why I told you what's going on with me.

- It's okay to say you can't support me in this, but it's not okay to shame me for seeking support. I trusted you by telling you I'm dealing with depression right now. Saying, "Don't be weak" is totally unhelpful.

"Did you take your meds?" "Aren't you supposed to have meds for that?" "Guess the meds aren't working!"

- Yes, I did take my meds, and I'm having a lot of depression symptoms today. It's normal for things to fluctuate, and if it goes too long like this, I will talk to my doctor about increasing my dose or something. What I need from you right now is a hug and to just listen to me share what's heavy on my heart. Okay?

- If you're trying to tease me about my mental health meds, it's not working. All I'm hearing is, "I don't know how to support you with your mental health, so I'm making a joke to try to relieve my discomfort about my own inadequacy right now." If that's not what you meant, please try again.

Belongings

When I left home at 17 years old, the first place I lived was with five roommates. Right when you entered our house, there was a mountain of shoes piled in the entryway. It was tripped over and added to whenever we had guests, and after I lived there for three weeks, I couldn't stand it anymore. I decided to organize the shoes.

It took hours.

I paired everything, grouped them by type, and then asked my roommates to please gather up their shoes to take back to their rooms.

What none of us expected was the 60-plus pairs of shoes left over that didn't belong to anyone currently living in the house! Lots of roommates had come and gone over the past few years, and between them and guests, there were so many abandoned pairs of shoes! I was shocked that nobody had taken responsibility to sort the communal pile of shoes until I moved in. Now, almost two decades later, I'm not shocked at all. People often assume everybody follows the same rules for individual and communal items, when actually what we think is okay and not okay varies widely.

Here are several scenarios and statements to help you say the thing when it comes to people moving, borrowing, or breaking your belongings.

MOVED BELONGINGS

They touched or moved your belongings.

- Please don't touch my stuff without asking first. It really bothers me.

- I know you're just trying to help clean up, but when you move my things and I don't know where you put them, it's really frustrating for me. Would you like to have a conversation about where things belong so you can put them away if you want to, and I can still find them later?

- I appreciate that your intent is to help me. That's very kind of you! Moving my stuff around in the kitchen isn't helpful, but what would be is if you ask me how you can help, and I'll give you some suggestions.

- I get that my stuff was in your way, and I'm sure that was really frustrating, so you moved it. In the future, if I'm at home, will you ask me to move it myself? All of this is kind of delicate, but I am more comfortable being the only one to touch my things. Thank you for understanding!

They threw away your stuff without checking with you first. When you asked what happened to your stuff, they said, "You don't need it, so I tossed it out for you."

- I understand your intention is to be helpful, but it feels disrespectful that you threw away my stuff without asking. Please don't do that again.

- We need to have a conversation about what is okay to throw away and what is not. Is now a good time for you to talk about that with me?

- I understand that the clutter bothers you, but if you're not able to resist throwing away my stuff when you're here, we'll have to meet up at other places, and I won't invite you to my home again.

BORROWED BELONGINGS

"But we're family! Family shares everything!"

- It's okay if you want to share everything with family members, but that's not something I am going to do.

- So far, "family shares everything" ends up with one person doing all the giving and everyone else receiving. I'm not participating in that anymore.

- I understand you're frustrated that I'm not giving you what you want, but I can't give extra when I don't have any. Please stop asking me.

- It feels like you're trying to guilt me into giving you something I already said I don't want to give. I hope I'm misunderstanding your point.

They borrow your belongings without asking.

- Hey! We need to have a conversation about what's okay to use without checking first and what I would prefer you ask me before borrowing. Is now a good time to talk about that?

- I get that everybody comes from different families with different rules about using each other's stuff. In my family growing up, you always asked before borrowing anything. After living with you for a bit, I'm realizing your family growing up probably borrowed stuff and then informed the person afterward. I'm having a hard time with that, even though I know you're not trying to hurt me and you've always done a great job of telling me when you borrowed something. Will you ask me before borrowing stuff from now on?

- I'm not okay with people borrowing my stuff. This is something I'm very particular about, so please don't take my things again.

- Did you borrow my [item]? I would really appreciate it if you would check with me before using my stuff. I needed it and when it wasn't where I had left it, I was really delayed with what I was trying to quickly accomplish. I'll usually say yes if you need to borrow something, it's just helpful to know that you have it and that I didn't lose it somewhere!

They borrowed your belongings and you have reminded them three times to return it, but they haven't yet.

- Hey! This is the fourth time I've asked you to give my book back. If you can't drop that off by tonight, will you send me the funds so I can buy a new one?

- I'm not sure why you haven't returned my drill yet. Maybe you're just exceptionally busy, so it's a hassle to drop it off, in which case I'd be happy to come pick it up. Does Tuesday or Wednesday after five work better for you?

- I know sometimes life gets in the way, so I've been as patient as I can be. But at this point, I've asked you multiple times to return the colander you borrowed last week because it's a part of my kitchen I use almost daily, and I need it back. What time today can you bring it by?

- I'm not going to be able to loan you anything ever again if you can't return the things you already borrowed!

BROKEN BELONGINGS

They touched, moved, or borrowed your belongings, and something got broken, damaged, or lost.

- I know it was an accident that the [item] you borrowed got broken. Stuff happens, and I get that. The part I'm having a hard time with is that you put it back without telling me it was broken. Why did you do that?

- When you moved my guitar and it got scratched, I know that was an accident. I'm not angry at you, but I would really appreciate an apology and an offer to get it fixed if possible.

- It's okay that you borrowed my hoodie. It's not okay that you borrowed it and lost it. I'm not comfortable with you borrowing my clothes again, at least until my hoodie is replaced.

- I was doing you a big favor when I loaned you my car. I'm pretty upset that it came back with a dent in the door that it didn't have before. What are you going to do to fix this?

They lost or damaged irreplaceable sentimental items.

- I'm pretty devastated that you lost Grandma's cameo brooch. She promised that to me before she died, and it's irreplaceable. I'm going to need space for a bit to work through my feelings about this.

- It is not okay that I asked you if the bedroom door was closed to keep the dog out and you said yes without checking, and now my childhood stuffy is in three pieces. I feel hurt and upset, because even if I sew her back together, Mrs. Muffins won't ever be the same. Will you please always check if the door is closed from now on?

- I'm trying to say this as calmly as possible because I understand it was an accident, but that's broken now beyond repair and I'm really sad. I need some time to grieve, and I'll let you know when I'm ready to connect again. Until then, please don't contact me.

They ruined your stuff, you asked them to pay to fix it, and they said no.

- Ultimately, it's your choice whether you pay for this or not, but this is going to change our relationship if you're not willing to take accountability to fix something you broke.

- I'm disappointed you're choosing not to repair what you damaged. If it's for financial reasons, I'm willing to work out a payment plan.

- This is a big deal to me, and I will need to get the legal system involved if we can't work this out between us.

- I have gone ahead and gotten in touch with my lawyer to get this resolved. You will be hearing from her.

"I didn't realize you would make such a big deal out of nothing. Stop overreacting."

- I'm having a proportionate response to you borrowing my laptop and then breaking it. That's really not okay.

- It might not be a big deal to you, but it is a big deal to me. Please stop trying to minimize my emotions.

- The fact that you are blaming me for my feelings instead of taking accountability for your actions is really concerning to me. A better option would be, "I'm sorry that I lost your necklace. What can I do to fix this?"

"Wow. I didn't realize you're so materialistic that you care more about stuff than people."

- It sounds like you're trying to deflect attention from what you broke by debating the validity of my feelings about it. I'm going to keep the focus of this conversation on how you can make this right again.

- It's possible to care about both stuff and people. They are not mutually exclusive. I care about you *and* I'm upset about the item you ruined.

Bodies

I once posed nude for a local art class who advertised for figure drawing models. I'd never been naked in what felt like public before and was a little nervous about being able to hold still for the length of time they requested.

Settled comfortably on a divan, I listened to music and the soft scrape of pencils on canvas for 30 minutes. At the first break, I walked around to see how the drawings were progressing.

One artist remarked, "I love drawing bodies like yours! They're so interesting! You're art!" as he gestured to the shadows and highlights on my fat rolls that he'd sketched.

As I sat for the next 30 minutes, nude in a room full of people looking intently at my body, I considered what he'd said. I'd previously tried the body positivity technique of declaring to myself, "My body is beautiful!" but it felt too far from my current belief of "My body is a problem."

The idea that my body is *interesting*? That I'm art? *My body is art?*

That was the bridge I needed! After that day, I've used "my body is art" as a mantra whenever I feel less than stellar about my lumps, bumps, moles, acne, and stray hairs.

Art doesn't have to be pretty or perfect. It can be grotesque or boring or maddening. As long as it makes you feel an emotion, it's art. And that's my body. I am art.

This chapter includes comments people make about bodies that are different from theirs. It's the top requested type of boundary script that I get from my clients: what to say when people comment on your body.

Now you can tell them, "I am art."

TALL

"Wow! You're so tall!"

- Candidly, I get that comment a lot, and it really just comes across as "You are different from everybody else," which doesn't feel good.

- I know you're just surprised, but I would appreciate it if you don't comment on my body.

"How's the weather up there?"

- I know you're trying to be funny, but that's the third time someone has said that to me this week, and I would appreciate it if you didn't say it again.

- Hey, I wanted to let you know that asking me "How's the weather up there?" every time I see you is getting kind of old. I like joking around with you, and I would appreciate it if you got some new material.

"Do you play basketball?"

- I get that you're just trying to make conversation, but asking a tall person if they play basketball is like asking a short person if they play miniature golf.

- Unless you're trying to organize a pickup game during lunch, I'm really not a fan of being asked if I play a particular sport just because of my body size.

"If you were skinnier, you could be a supermodel!"

- Isn't that kind of an odd thing to say to someone you don't know very well? Like, "Hey! You could have a totally different career if you looked totally different!"

- I think you meant that as a compliment, but it came across as fat shaming. Please don't comment on my body.

- A better option is to compliment something I've chosen, like my shoes, instead of my height, which is something genetic that I cannot control.

SHORT

"Wow! You're so short!"

- I know you're just surprised, but I would appreciate it if you didn't comment on my body.

- That might be the first time you've ever said that, but that's the third time I've heard it today. Please don't comment on my height.

They use the top of your head as an armrest.

- I know you're trying to be funny, but I seriously don't like that. Please don't do that again.

- I'd rather not have my face so close to your armpit. Please don't use my head as an armrest again.

"My eight-year-old child is taller than you!"

- I know you're just making a light-hearted remark, but I don't like being told I look like a child. Please don't say that again.
- I don't enjoy being compared to a child, even one as wonderful as I'm sure your eight-year-old is.

"Can you even drive? How do you reach the pedals?"

- Yes, I can drive. Why do you ask?
- Are you asking for a ride somewhere and wondering if I can drive you?

OLD

"Do you even know what [brand-new technology] is?"

- Are you really asking me if I'm familiar with that technology, or is this just a roundabout way of saying I seem really old to you?
- Yes, I do know what that is. Why do you ask?

"When I get that old, shoot me."

- Wow. That's a violently unkind thing to say about someone.
- That comment seems out of character for you. Why would you say that?

"Boomer!"

- If I did something to upset you, please just say that. There's no need to insult my age.

- I understand that you're frustrated with me, but there's no need to call names.

"You have a good body for someone your age!"

- I know you meant that as a compliment, but I would prefer it if you didn't comment on my body.

- I have a personal rule that I don't discuss my body with anyone but my doctors and my lovers, so let's talk about something else!

YOUNG

"You're just a baby!"

- I know finding out how young I am brought up your feelings about your own age, but I don't appreciate being called a baby.

- I get that you're making a joke, but I don't like being teased about my age, so let's find something else to laugh about, okay?

"Are you even old enough to work here?"

- Yes, I absolutely am. I have more experience than you might guess!

- I think your intention is to be funny, but the joke's not landing, so let's move on, okay?

"You're too young to be tired!"

- I know we're all just joking around, but your repeated comments about how I'm "too young to be tired" are starting to wear thin. I'd appreciate it if you knock it off.

- I understand that you meant it in a friendly way, but saying, "You're too young to be tired" just sounds like "You're lazy for taking a break," which doesn't feel good. A better option would be, "I hope you enjoy your break!"

"How old are you?"

- Why do you ask?

- Is there an age requirement I wasn't aware of?

THIN

"You're so skinny! Are you anorexic?"

- No. That's not okay to say to someone. You have no idea what's happening with someone's health, and asking if they have an eating disorder is really unkind.

- Are you trying to start a conversation about my health? Because that wasn't a good way to go about it. A better option is saying, "I'm worried about your health. Can we talk about that?"

- I promise that everyone who needs to know my private medical information already does know. You're not on that short list, so I'm not discussing my health with you.

"You should eat something."

- Please don't comment on my body size. It makes me uncomfortable.

- It's not fun to have people comment on how skinny I am all the time. I'd appreciate it if you would stop the body-size comments.

"You look like you'd blow away in a strong wind!"

- I know you're saying that to be funny, but it just sounds like "The only way I know how to connect with you is by making inappropriate comments on your body size." It's okay to just talk about the weather or ask me how my weekend was instead.

- I get that you're joking, but my body size isn't something I have a sense of humor around, so can we find something else to laugh about?

"Real women have curves."

- I'm not sure what your intention is in saying that, but it comes across as "I think you have less value to men because of your body type." Is that what you're trying to say?

- It sounds like you're saying, "You're not a real woman" or "You're too skinny to be a real woman." That hurts my feelings. Women have a wide variety of body types!

"You look like a skeleton with skin!"

- Whoa. That's a shockingly unkind thing to say to someone.

- Well, if your goal is to hurt my feelings, you've succeeded! You don't ever really know what's going on with someone's body or health, so comparing them to "a skeleton with skin" is just an awful thing to say.

FAT

See *Fatness & Food* on page 133.

HAIR

"Can I touch your hair?"

- No. Absolutely not. I am not an animal in a petting zoo.

- I'm here to work, not to satisfy your curiosity about textured hair.

"Is that your real hair?"

- I get that you're curious, but that is a very personal question, and I am not going to answer.

- I know this isn't how you meant it, but that is a stereotypical question that racist people will ask people of color, especially, Black women, so it's better to google it if you are curious.

"Nobody wants to see armpit hair. It's gross."

- I do! That's why I have it! If you don't want to see it, you're welcome not to look.

- I disagree, and I don't appreciate you saying that the natural hair that grows out of my body is gross.

"You should shave your legs."

- I am happy with how I am managing my leg hair. If I wanted to change it, I would.

- It's okay for you to have an aesthetic preference
  for how you want your own leg hair to be
  and what length of leg hair you find the most
  attractive on others. It's not okay to tell me
  what to do with my body.

"Does the carpet match the drapes?"

- What does that mean?

- What an odd thing to say to a stranger! Why
  are you asking me about my pubic hair? That's
  literally none of your business.

"Nobody will hire you with your blue hair."

- Unless I'm specifically asking you to hire me
  for a job, your opinion on my hair color isn't
  relevant or helpful.

- I know you're saying that because you're
  concerned about my job prospects. Please trust
  that I am an adult who knows what I'm doing,
  and I've decided to have blue hair, even if some
  people don't like it.

- Personally, I'm not interested in ever working
  somewhere that judges my professional
  qualifications on my hair color!

"Why don't you have any eyelashes?" "Why do you have bald patches?" "What happened to your eyebrows?" (This is often said to those who have trichotillomania or other hair-loss conditions.)

- I have a disorder that affects my hair. It's not
  contagious, and I'm getting help for it. I would
  appreciate it if you didn't mention my bald

patches again because it's something I'm pretty sensitive about.

- It's actually really personal and not something I'm comfortable talking about. Please respect my privacy and don't bring it up again.

"Look at that hairline! You're definitely going bald."

- I know you're just teasing me, but I'm actually pretty sensitive about my hair loss, and I would prefer it if you didn't mention it.

- Hey, would you do me a favor and not talk about my receding hairline? Thanks.

ACNE

"You'd be so pretty if you didn't have that acne!"

- Wow. "You'd be so pretty if . . ." is quite the backhanded compliment.

- That is not a helpful or kind thing to say. Please don't mention my acne again.

"Have you tried [product name]?"

- It's one thing if I ask you for a product recommendation, and it's another thing if you start handing out unsolicited advice about skin care products. Please wait for me to ask for your expertise before giving it.

- I know your intention is to be helpful, but I'm not in a space to discuss my skin care routine right now. Let's talk about something else.

"Aren't you a little old to have acne like that?"

- Adult acne is pretty common, especially as a medication side effect or when hormones fluctuate during menstruation or menopause. This means some people get acne all the way into their 50s, so, no, there's no such thing as being "a little old to have acne."

- Are you asking because you're expressing concern for my skin but saying it in an awkward way, or are you actually curious about what causes adult acne?

"Maybe you should stop eating greasy food!"

- That's a myth! Oily foods do not cause oily skin; hormones do! So while I appreciate the concern, I promise I know what I'm doing.

- I know that your intention is to be helpful by sharing what you believe is good skin care advice, but there's actually not a correlation between greasy food and acne. I would appreciate it if you didn't mention my skin again unless I brought it up first.

MOLES

"You'd be prettier if you had those moles taken care of."

- I don't think you're insulting me on purpose, but that's definitely how it's coming across. It's like you're giving a backhanded compliment, so I'll feel insecure. It's not working, but it is annoying. Please stop commenting on my appearance.

- What an odd thing to say. Unless somebody directly asks you, "Do you think I would be prettier if I had my moles removed?" it's really none of your business.

"Cindy Crawford can do a facial mole. You can't."

- I didn't ask for your opinion of my face. Please keep your thoughts to yourself.

- Wow. That is blatantly insulting.

- If your intention was to hurt my feelings, you failed. But if your intention was to show off how rude you can be, you've definitely succeeded.

SCARS

"What happened to your arms?"

- Oh, it happened a long time ago. I don't like to talk about it, so let's move on to another topic.

- They're scars. Why do you ask?

"You'll never be able to wear a bikini with a scar like that!"

- People with scars wear bikinis all the time!

- I'm not sure what your intention was with that comment, but it came across like, "Your body is too disfigured to be shown in public, so you better cover up." If that's not what you meant, will you clarify what you were trying to say?

"Those marks are unprofessional. You should cover them up."

- Humans have scars after they get hurt. There's nothing inherently unprofessional about them. I'm offended you would even say that!

- Just because you are uncomfortable with how my body looks, doesn't make my body "unprofessional." Please don't comment on my scars again.

"Wow. That's a gnarly scar! Did you lose a fight with a bear?"

- I get that you're just trying to make conversation, but I actually don't like talking about my scars. Tell me about the game instead. What was the final score?

- I don't answer strangers' questions about my body. Thank you for respecting my privacy.

WRINKLES

"Have you tried [product name] for those crow's feet wrinkles?"

- I'm not open to unsolicited advice about my face right now. If that changes, I'll let you know.

- I'm really happy that I have smile lines by my eyes or "crow's feet," as you called them! I have no interest in getting rid of them. I think they're a sign that I've lived a life full of laughter!

"You would look so much younger with Botox!"

- First, I didn't ask for your advice on looking younger. Second, please don't comment on my facial appearance again.

- I get that you're just trying to be helpful, but this is actually not a topic I have any chill about, so we should talk about something else before I get on my soapbox about the importance of allowing our bodies to age naturally.

"You look like a grandma with all those wrinkles."

- Considering that my grandma was one of my favorite people in the world, I'm gonna take that as a compliment!

- I probably won't ever be a grandma since I don't have kids, but I'm happy to look like one. Grandmas are awesome!

"My cousin got a facelift and has never looked better! Have you considered that?"

- Please don't give me any advice about my appearance unless I specifically ask you first. Thank you.

- I know you're just trying to be helpful, but what you just said really came across as "You look terrible and need surgical intervention to improve your appearance." That is pretty insulting, and I would appreciate it if you didn't make comments like that again.

TATTOOS

"Tattoos aren't attractive on women."

- What makes you think I'm trying to attract you?

- I didn't ask for your opinion on my body art, and I would appreciate it if you kept your thoughts to yourself.

They touch your tattoo without asking.

- Hold up! Please don't touch me without asking.

- [Grab their hand or duck away] Oops! I know you're just admiring my beautiful body art, but I really don't like being touched by strangers.

"You'll regret it when you're older."

- I'm confident that at the end of my life I won't regret the beautiful tattoos I have, and I'll be glad I wasn't worried about other people's opinions.

- I would rather risk regretting decorating myself with gorgeous body art then risk regretting that I didn't.

"I would never disfigure myself like that."

- Nobody's going to hold you down and force you to get a tattoo. Just because it's not something you would choose doesn't mean it's not okay for other people to choose that.

- It's okay to know that tattoos aren't your thing, but it's not okay to tell someone they've "disfigured" themselves. That's incredibly unkind.

PIERCINGS & BODY MODIFICATIONS

"You're ruining your body."

- I can decorate my body however I want. Your approval is not required.

- I understand that you care about me and you're concerned about the ways I have changed my appearance. If you want to have a conversation about your fears that I'm "ruining my body," a better way to start that would be asking, "I'm having some feelings about your new body mods and piercings. Can we talk about that?"

"Do you have any piercings in *other* places?"

- It's pretty weird to ask a stranger about their genitals. I'm not going to answer that question.

- The only people who need to know what's happening in my pants are my doctor and my lovers. You don't fit either category, so I'm not talking about that with you.

"I can't believe you would willingly do that to yourself."

- One of the things I love about body modifications is people have been doing them for over 5,000 years! This is an ancient tradition that I am happily participating in.

- Just because piercings are not your thing doesn't give you permission to make snarky comments. Please keep your judgments to yourself.

"Aren't you worried people will think that you self-harm/ are mentally ill/are a criminal?"

- I have a really short list of people whose opinions I care about, and everybody on that list knows the truth about me. I don't make decisions based on what people who are not on my shortlist will think about me.

- When you say "People will think harsh judgments about you someday," it kind of sounds like you're saying, "I'm thinking harsh judgments about you right now." Is that what you meant?

Children,
Child-Free, Fertility,
& Pregnancy

My mom went to her 10-year high school reunion and received the trophy for "Most Children" in her graduating class. The five of us girls laughed really hard when she told us because at the time our neighbors had 10 kids and a family on the next block had 14 kids!

I grew up in a community of big families. I have years of babysitting and live-in nanny experience. I think kids are wonderful! However, I am not raising kids and I only work with adults as a boundary coach. This chapter contains boundary phrases for parents and caregivers to use when speaking to other adults about your children. *These are not boundary phrases for children to say.*

If your goal is to teach boundary phrases to your children, my recommendation is to get really proficient at saying the thing yourself, and your children will learn from your example.

FERTILITY

"When are you having kids? The clock is ticking!"

- That's a really common question that I personally don't like being asked. I know you didn't mean any harm, but please don't bring up when I'm having kids again.

- I get that your intent is to be kind, but that question just sounds like, "Have you given up hope yet? You're getting too old!" And it upsets me. Unless I bring up my baby-making timeline with you, please don't mention it to me again.

- I know you're excited for me and I appreciate that, but I don't discuss my fertility with anyone besides my partner(s) and my medical professionals.

"Why haven't you given me grandbabies yet?"

- I know how important the idea of grandbabies is to you. I can't give you any idea on if or when that might happen, so I would appreciate it if you didn't bring it up again until I mention it myself.

- I've told you before and I'm telling you again now: I'm not having children. Your choices are to accept that, or we can keep having this awkward conversation over and over. I'd definitely prefer you accept it and not keep asking me when I've already given you my final answer on the subject.

- I appreciate how much you love your grandbabies and want more of them! It hurts me to keep being asked that question because it sounds like, "Why are you a failure?" I promise when there is any news, I'll tell you! But until then, please don't keep asking me.

"When are you having another one?"

- Why do you ask?

- My partner(s) and I are really happy with our family size.

- I know you're asking because you're curious and you care about me and my family. The frequent question about having another baby is starting to come across like, "The children you have now aren't enough." Please don't ask me that again.

"You have a lot of kids! You know what causes that, right?"

- I know you're saying that as a joke, but your commenting on my sex life is awkward to me, and I'd appreciate it if you didn't say stuff like that to me.

- I love having a big family! I'm really happy to be the parent of so many wonderful tiny humans!

INFERTILITY

"I can't believe you're spending that much on IVF!"

- Some people invest in stocks or small businesses. This is what our family has decided to invest in.

- This is what works for me. It's not my favorite thing to talk about, so let's switch topics. How did it go with your car repair?
- I'm not going to discuss my family finances with you.

"Why don't you just adopt?"

- That's not an option for our family. Please don't bring that up again.

- I know you're saying that to be helpful, but casually suggesting a seemingly simplistic solution to a complex problem isn't okay with me. What would be helpful is if we change the topic. Thanks.

- People feel a lot of different ways about adoption. That is not a conversation I'm interested in having right now.

"Miscarriage happens all the time. It's not like it was a real baby."

- It's okay to say you're not comfortable talking about miscarriage with me. It's not okay to shame me for grieving the loss of my wanted pregnancy. What you just said was incredibly unkind.

- Yes, miscarriages are common. Your views on if a fetus counts as a baby aren't what I need to hear right now. Please either apologize for the hurtful thing you just said or leave, and I'll let you know when I'm ready to talk to you again.

- When something I really looked forward to doesn't happen, I deserve to grieve. It's not okay to shift your discomfort with my sadness into downplaying what happened. That's mean.

Your friend is pregnant and wants you to be involved in celebrating, but you're not emotionally okay doing that because of your complex feelings about your own infertility.

- Thank you for inviting me to the baby shower! I'm really excited for you and your partner(s)! I won't be able to attend, but I am sending my gift along with Astrid. I hope you have fun!

- I appreciate you asking me to celebrate your new baby joy with you. I'm grieving a pregnancy loss right now so I'm not going to be there, but I am really happy for you and your wife! I'm looking forward to baby pictures when they're available!

- I didn't tell you before, but I'm dealing with some infertility stuff right now, so I'm not in the right headspace to help you plan a pregnancy celebration. I hope it's really fun, and once I'm feeling better I'd love to hear all about it!

PREGNANCY

"Are you pregnant?"

- No. Are you?

- I know you're just curious, but I have a personal rule that I don't discuss my body with strangers. Thank you for understanding.

- Why do you ask? Is there a safety requirement I'm not aware of?

"Is it a boy or a girl?"

- It's a baby! We won't know what their gender is until they tell us.

- I know that's a common question to ask pregnant people, but I don't like speculating about my baby's gender. Thank you for respecting our privacy.

- That's not a question I'm going to answer. But I will tell you that we're expecting the baby in November. I'm so excited to have another Scorpio in the family!

They touch your stomach without asking you.

- WHOA. Please don't touch me!

- I'm not okay with you touching me. Please remove your hand right now.

- [Touch their stomach back] Oh, I thought we were rubbing bellies!

"Wow! You're huge!" "You look like you're about to pop!" "Are you sure you don't have three babies in there?"

- I know you're just surprised at how much I've grown since you saw me last, but I'm feeling pretty sensitive about my size right now. I'd prefer you say "You're glowing" or "What can I do to support you? Would you like some water or juice?"

- I get that you're making conversation and don't mean any harm, but that sounds like a criticism and not a celebration. Please don't comment about my size again. Thank you.

CHILDREN

"I never let my kids act like that in public!"

- I know you just said that to your friend, but it's obvious you're commenting on my child and me. It's not helpful when a parent is having a hard time to criticize from the sidelines. Please consider being kinder to the strangers you see out in public.

- Okay. Good for you. Please excuse me so I can focus on my child.

- Are you trying to help the situation? Because that's not helpful. What would be helpful is if you offered a cup of water or a tissue right now. Or just walked away.

"Why is he acting like that?"

- I'm not going to answer curious questions right now. I'm busy parenting. Thanks!

- He is a tiny human, and sometimes humans get upset. It's a normal part of social and emotional development.

- I know you're concerned, but I've got this. Thanks, though!

"Some people just shouldn't have children."

- Judging strangers for their parenting is a pretty low game.

- I think it's easy to criticize when you don't have all the context.

- Wow. What an unkind thing to say.

"Why don't you just spank her?"

- I don't need suggestions, especially ones like that. I've got this!

- Not that it's any of your business, but we don't hit each other in our family. Hurting people when they need care isn't something I'm okay with.

CHILD-FREE

"Why don't you want kids?"

- For the same reasons that people do want kids! It's the lifestyle and future that will make me happiest.

- I know you're asking because you're curious, but this isn't a topic I discuss at work. Thank you for respecting my privacy.

- I believe children deserve to be raised by people who 100 percent want them! Since I don't 100 percent want them, I'm choosing not to have them. To me, this is the most loving choice I can make.

"Who will take care of you when you're old?"

- Are you trying to start a conversation about retirement investments? Because a better way to ask that is, "What are your retirement plans?"

- Have you heard about those people who live on cruise ships until they die? I'm thinking something like that!

- I know you're asking because you care and are worried about me. I'm okay; I've already got it all figured out with my estate attorney.

"Oh, so you hate kids?"

- I love elephants, but that doesn't mean I want to change my lifestyle to keep one at my home. It's possible to love something you're not interested in taking care of every day.

- I like kids as much as I like adults: on a case-by-case basis.

- *Hate* is too strong of a word, but, yes, I dislike children in general. I like some of my friend's kids, but that's about it.

"You must be so lonely. I can't imagine life without my kids."

- I know you're saying that because you care, but, candidly, you don't know me well enough to determine if I'm lonely or not.

- I appreciate the concern, but I'm a big believer in different strokes for different folks. It's possible that what makes me happiest would make you miserable and vice versa.

Disability

I'm disabled, and most of my loved ones are disabled. We get a lot of curious and well-intentioned but ultimately rude questions and comments from non-disabled people. The most common one is, "You're supposed to say 'person with disabilities' not 'disabled person.'" or some other form of language policing like, "You're not disabled; you're differently abled!"

No.

I use identity-first language and describe myself as a "disabled person" instead of using person-first language like "person with disabilities." I refuse to separate myself from my needs and challenges because I am not ashamed of them. I'm not the problem; society is. I feel like person-first language like "person with a disability" is implying if you weren't carrying that pesky disability around, you'd fit into society great! Like I'm supposed to hide that I need accommodations to exist or else I will be judged to be bizarre, broken, or abnormal.

Again, no.

I'm proud of my identity as a disabled person. I'm proud to be part of the disability community. Within that community are both hidden and visible disabilities. Hidden disabilities are those you won't notice just by looking at the person, like epilepsy, diabetes, ADHD, dyslexia, schizophrenia, etc. Visible disabilities are those you will notice by looking at the person, like limb differences, paralysis, Down's Syndrome, blindness, cerebral palsy, etc.

Currently most of my disabilities are of the hidden variety. Autism, obsessive disorder, depression, PTSD, and CPTSD. My visible disability is that I'm fat.

You might be thinking, "I don't think all of those count as disabilities." Or "If those are disabilities, then I'm disabled too, and I don't know how I feel about that." I understand. Claiming your identity as a disabled person is complex. I encourage you to define disability in whatever way works for you. My personal definition of a disability is: Does having this condition require accommodations to exist in society? Yes? Then that's a disability.

With hidden disabilities, the social challenge is when people don't understand or agree that accommodations are necessary for the disabled person. They might say things like, "Get over it" or "You're exaggerating for attention."

With visible disabilities, the social challenge is when people feel entitled to private medical information because they're curious about how the disabled person is different from non-disabled people. "What happened to you?" or "How do you have sex?"

This chapter includes questions and comments that I and my disabled loved ones have gotten, as well as submissions from my clients and students. They are grouped by general ableism, intellectual/developmental disabilities, physical disabilities, and sensory disabilities.

Please note that there are separate chapters for ADHD and autism, fatness, and anxiety and depression.

GENERAL ABLEISM

"You're supposed to say 'person with a disability' not 'disabled person.'"

- You're referring to identity-first versus person-first language. I choose to use identity-first language.

- As a disabled person, I get to choose how I want to refer to myself, and I prefer "disabled person."

- I appreciate that you're advocating for disabled people. There's differences of opinion on whether person-first or identity-first language is better. I personally choose to use identity-first language.

- That may be what you learned at some point, but in my experience as a disabled person, the majority of disabled people prefer identity-first language.

"You're so inspiring!" "You're so brave!" "You're so special!"

- Are you saying that I am brave for existing as a disabled person? I know you mean that as a compliment, but it comes across as very hurtful.

- I know you meant that in the kindest way possible, but telling a disabled person they're "so inspiring" for doing everyday regular stuff like going to the grocery store comes across as othering.

- If you wouldn't say it to a non-disabled person doing the same thing, then don't say it to a disabled person.

- I get that you're trying to be nice, but all I'm hearing is "I don't see you as a whole person like me."

"The only real disability is a bad attitude!"

- No amount of positive thinking is going to turn stairs into a wheelchair-accessible ramp.

- As a disabled person (or someone who has disabled friends and family), that has not been my experience, and I actually find that expression pretty offensive. Please don't say that around me again.

"Are we inclusive? Sure! We hired one of 'those people.'" [Referring to a disabled person]

- I know you didn't mean it this way, but referring to disabled people as "those people" is offensive. Please choose different language.

- Hmm. May I offer you some feedback on something it seems like you don't know yet? [They consent to receive feedback.] I really appreciate that you are inclusive, and I think it's awesome that you have a disabled person on your team. But when you refer to disabled people as "those people," it comes across as "I don't see them as human as I am." I know that's not what you meant at all, so a better option in the future would be saying "disabled people" or "Our team includes both disabled and non-disabled people."

They use the r-word.

- That's a slur. Don't say that around me again.

- I know that's a word that was common back in the day, but it's now considered an offensive slur and is not appropriate to say when referring to disabled people. You can say "disabled" or "has a developmental disorder." But don't say the r-word.

They whisper the word *disabled* when saying, "She is, you know, 'disabled.'"

- You don't need to whisper. Disabilities are nothing to be ashamed of.

- I think your intention is to be polite, but when you whisper the word *disability*, it comes across as though you're ashamed or embarrassed that they're disabled. Also, it's okay to refer to someone's disability at a normal speaking volume.

"I wouldn't ever date someone disabled like you."

- Unless we're specifically having a conversation where I asked you to date me, that's a really odd thing to say.

- I don't know if you're going to be able to receive this, but I'm going to try saying it anyway. Everyone will eventually either become disabled or die. Someday you might have an accident, develop a health condition, or just get old! When you're judging someone's disability status, please consider that you will also most likely become disabled someday.

"Your partner is such an angel to take care of you!"

- I know you meant that as a compliment to my partner, and I agree with you that they are really great! The way you phrased it came across as, "I'm amazed that somebody would choose to be in a relationship with a disabled person." A better option would be, "I can tell you're really happy together." Or "You seem like a really great team!"

- I think your intention was to be kind but that sounded like, "Your partner is a superior being for putting up with your disabilities!" which is not kind.

INTELLECTUAL & DEVELOPMENTAL DISABILITIES

"Are you stupid?"

- Why do you ask? Do you need help with something?

- If your intention is to assess my intellect, you've succeeded. If your intention is to insult me, you've failed.

"You've said that three times in the last five minutes."

- It's okay to remind me that I've repeated myself. It's not okay to raise your voice and be unkind to me.

- I understand that me repeating myself is frustrating. If you need to take a break from this conversation, that's okay. What's not okay is treating me like I'm stupid because my memory isn't what it used to be.

They use "baby talk" when speaking to disabled adults.

- I don't understand what you're saying. Will you repeat it without the baby talk, please?

- Hold on! I think you've confused me with a small child. I'm an adult, and I'd prefer for you to speak to me like an adult.

They are horrified that disabled adults drink alcohol.

- Adults drink alcohol. Why are you so surprised?

- I appreciate that you really care about me and I value our relationship, so I need to tell you: your shock that I, an adult, drink alcohol sometimes comes across like you think I'm a child. I am disabled, but that doesn't mean I can't do typical adult activities. Would you be shocked if a non-disabled adult my age drank a beer?

They are horrified that disabled adults have sex.

- I understand that it's uncomfortable for you to think that I have sex because in your mind, I'm like a child. But that's your issue to work through, not mine.

- It's okay to say that you don't want to talk about my sex life with me. It's not okay to express horror or disgust that I have sex, which is something adults my age often do.

PHYSICAL DISABILITIES

"What happened to you?"

- I'm not going to answer that.

- I don't share my private medical information with strangers.

- I don't talk about my disabilities in public.

- My body is not your business.

- I get that you're curious and just asking, but this is the third time today somebody has questioned me about my body. I am not in the mood to share my painful health history with you right now.

"How do you go to the bathroom?"

- Just because you're curious doesn't mean I owe you an explanation about how my body works.

- I appreciate that you are curious. I'm happy to answer specific questions about my accommodation needs at work, but I'm not going to educate you on information you can easily find online.

"How do you have sex?"

- It's kind of weird that you're asking me for the birds and the bees talk right now.

- Oh, I'm not a sex ed teacher. I'm not going to answer that for you.

"You're faking it! I saw you stand up from your wheelchair!"

- Ambulatory wheelchair users exist. Not everybody who has a wheelchair is paralyzed.

- Wow. What a genuinely unkind thing to say.

- I'm not going to educate you on all the reasons why somebody uses a wheelchair, but paralysis is just one of them. That doesn't mean all other wheelchair users are "faking it."

- What you just said is not okay, but we need to have a good working relationship, so I'm going to explain this to you. There are a lot of people who use wheelchairs, not because they can't walk but because if they do, they will be so exhausted that it defeats the purpose of going at all. Please don't accuse a wheelchair user of "faking it" ever again.

"The building doesn't have an elevator, but we do have big, strong men who can carry you up the stairs!"

- I know you meant that offer in a kind way, but all I'm hearing is "this building is not accessible."

- Please don't say that an event is "accessible" if the accessibility relies on me being physically lifted into the air by strangers. No thank you.

SENSORY
PROCESSING DISORDERS

"You think the lights are 'too bright'? They're just regular fluorescent lights!"

- I have a sensory processing disorder, which means I perceive sensory input differently than you do. To me, the lights are too bright.

- I'm pretty sure you meant that in a surprised way, but how you phrased it comes across as "you're a weirdo." Please believe me when I tell you how I'm experiencing the world even if it's different from your experience.

"You can hear the fridge humming from all the way over here? Yeah, right."

- Just because you can't hear it doesn't mean I can't. Not all people experience sounds the same way.

- I would really appreciate it if you believed me about how I hear the world. Being able to hear machines' electricity is part of my sensory processing disorder.

"You're being too sensitive. I can't smell anything."

- I am sensitive, and that smell is really bothering me. If I could ignore it, I would. Can we please turn on the fan?

- Am I too sensitive, or are you insensitive? Since I can't turn my nose off, my options are to change the environment or leave.

"Stop chewing on the pens! That's so gross! Why do you chew on everything?"

- Chewing on pens is a form of stimming, which is a self-soothing behavior. I'm happy to divide the pens into yours and mine so you have unchewed pens to write with because I'm probably never going to stop chewing on my pens.

- Chewing feels good and relaxes me. Where can we put pens that are just yours that I won't chew on?

"What do you mean the food hurts your mouth? Stop being such a baby!"

- Different people experience foods differently. I get that you're frustrated, but it's not okay to call me names.

- Just because it's not happening to you doesn't mean it's not happening to me. If it's too difficult for you to be around me with the way I eat, let's pick a different activity to do together instead of going out to dinner.

"It's not my fault you're so high maintenance."

- It sounds like you're frustrated that I have a lot of accommodation needs. I get if you need to take a break to get some space from me, but it's not okay to blame me for how you're feeling.

- I'm not sure what your intention was, but what you just said came across like you're angry at me for being disabled and inconveniencing you. If that's not what you meant, will you please clarify what you are saying?

DEAFNESS, HARD OF HEARING, & HEARING AIDS

They yell in your ear.

- Please don't yell at me. If I need you to speak up, I will ask.

- I think you were just trying to be funny by "testing my deafness" and yelling in my ear. That's not something I have a sense of humor about, so if you're trying to make me laugh, it isn't working.

You don't hear the person and ask them to repeat what was said. They say "Never mind" or "I don't want to repeat myself."

- I understand it's frustrating to repeat yourself. When you tell me "never mind," it comes across as "I'm not willing to make an effort to include you in the conversation." And I feel sad and left out. I would really appreciate it if you would repeat yourself when I don't hear you the first time.

- You were trying to tell me something, and I want to know what it was. You can choose not to repeat yourself, and then we will both be frustrated, or you can tell me what you said and we can move on with the conversation.

"He's in special ed, right?" [About your child with hearing aids]

- No, he's in a general education classroom. Hearing aids don't indicate any other disabilities besides difficulty hearing.

- I don't share details about my child with strangers. Thank you for respecting his privacy.

"I can't understand anything he says. Can you just tell me?"

- No. I don't speak on his behalf unless he asks me to. How would you feel if I asked someone else to speak for you?

- Yes, I can, but it's not going to help you communicate effectively in the future. A better option is to ask him to slow down and then try again.

- I'm not going to do that. You could write it down, use sign language, or try a communication app on your phone, but asking me to speak for him is not okay.

They equate deafness to stupidity.

- Just because I'm hard of hearing doesn't mean I'm hard of thinking. Please don't treat me like I'm stupid.

- I don't think you're doing it on purpose, but once you found out I am deaf, you switched to interacting with me like I'm a small child instead of an adult. It's kind of weird, and I'd appreciate it if you didn't do that anymore.

BLINDNESS, LOW VISION, & GLASSES

"How do you get dressed or put makeup on?"

- I get that you're just curious, but a better option than asking a stranger about their disability is looking it up online.

- That's not a question I'm going to answer. I deserve medical privacy.

"Wow! Those are thick glasses! Do you have to wear them at night to see your dreams?"

- I know that your intention is to be funny, but my glasses are not something I have a sense of humor about.

- I know you meant that as a joke, but it came across like bullying. In the future, please don't comment on my glasses.

"Have you tried contacts? You would look a lot better in contacts!"

- I know you're asking because you care about me, but what you just said came across as "You look really ugly with your glasses."

- I think it's one thing if I bring it up and ask you for your opinion on me wearing contacts versus glasses, but it's a very different thing for you to come up to me and say, "Change your face so I think you look more attractive."

STUTTERING & SPEECH DISABILITIES

"I don't have all day!"

- Please be patient with my disability.

- The more you yell at me, the more stressed I become, and the longer this takes.

"Just spit it out!"

- Wow. You are very impatient.

- I get that you're frustrated, but it's not okay to yell at me.

They slow down how they speak to you after hearing you stutter.

- Just because I speak slowly doesn't mean you need to.
- I understand you just fine. You don't need to slow down the way you speak to me.

Environment

One of my extended family members invented a renewable energy source using magnets. He got several generous offers from large energy companies wanting to buy the technology. According to family lore, when asked why he didn't accept their money, he said he was concerned they would suppress his invention instead of producing it because it competes with their current business model.

I think about that whenever the topic of the environment comes up. What is the responsibility of the individual? To reuse cloth shopping bags instead of single use plastic? To sort out recyclable items from trash? To not sell your renewable energy invention for buckets of money if you can't trust who you'd be selling it to?

I see a lot of blaming individuals for not doing enough to help the environment when I think most of the blame belongs to corporations and governments. I also support doing what you can as an individual or local community. The phrases below are to give you responses for when the environment conversation gets heated. (Yes, that was a global warming joke!)

"The climate isn't really changing!" "Recycling doesn't do anything." "I don't believe there are microplastics in the water. It's just another thing made up to scare people."

- Are you trying to start a debate? Because this is not something I'm going to argue about with you.

- I put my energy toward initiatives that help the environment, not into arguments with climate change deniers.

- I disagree. However, you sound very sure of that and are unlikely to change your mind, so let's talk about something else.

- Are you trying to start a conversation about this? There's a lot of basic information available online that you would need to know before we could dive deeper on these topics.

"There's nothing we can do about the environment, so we might as well enjoy ourselves!"

- I really disagree with that ideology. Are you open to some information that might change your mind, or should we switch topics to something else?

- I'm really surprised to hear you say that because I know you're someone who values family. I would've assumed you care about sustainable practices to help the next generation!

- You're right that global warming and the environmental crisis can feel really overwhelming and hopeless. May I share some good news with you about rewilding that's happening in Europe right now? I believe there's lots of hope and lots we can do about the environment while also enjoying ourselves.

"There's no such thing as ethical consumption under capitalism."

- That expression means corporations are having a bigger impact on the environment than individuals. It's not a justification to ignore sustainable practices.

- I'm not clear what that expression means to you. To me, it means people who are hustling to survive are not to blame for wearing fast fashion or using disposable plastics. The fault lies with capitalist corporations.

- It's not "perfectly ethical" or "not ethical at all." There's nuance and range. Maybe your food comes in disposable plastic, but you use a menstrual cup instead of throwing away tampons or pads every month. I think as individuals we're doing the best we can, and the ultimate responsibility is with corporations and governments.

Fatness & Food

I was at a backyard barbecue hosted by a friend of mine who was the only person there that I knew. I'd gone up to the picnic table and filled a plate, including some delicious-looking potato salad.

I sat down on a folding chair under a shady tree, balancing my plate on my knees, and went to take a bite. Across from me was an older woman that I didn't know. She looked at my food and said, "Are you sure you should be eating that?"

"Why?" I replied. "Is there something wrong with it?" I thought maybe ants had gotten into the potato salad or she saw one of the little kids stick their fingers in it.

"You know." She paused and looked me up and down. "It's *fattening.*"

Startled, I started to laugh. "Oh no! We don't make comments about people's bodies like that! That's so inappropriate!" I kept chuckling loudly to myself as I took a bite of the yummy potato salad. The woman stood up and walked away.

What an audacious thing for her to say! Perhaps she was trying to be helpful and went about it the wrong way. Perhaps she has a lot of anti-fat beliefs and was projecting onto me. Who knows! I'm grateful that I knew what to say to her rude comment, and with the statements in this chapter, now you will too!

FATNESS

"You're fat. You should lose weight."

- My body is not your business.

- Yes, I'm fat. I like my body exactly how it is.

- Nope! I'm not interested in shrinking myself for your approval.

- Oh! Don't talk about people's bodies that way. That's inappropriate.

- Unless I ask you for feedback on my body, please keep your comments to yourself.

"Moo! You look like a cow!"

- Cows are magnificent beasts, and I'm totally okay with being compared to them. Did you know some cultures consider them sacred?

- If your intention is to hurt me, you've failed. If your intention is to sound like a playground bully, you've succeeded.

"You're so brave to wear that!"

- I know you mean that as a compliment, but the subtext of what you just said is, "You should be uncomfortable wearing that because you're fat."

- I don't think it's your intention to imply I shouldn't wear this because I'm fat. A better compliment would be, "I love that color on you!" or "That's a beautiful pattern on your bikini!"

- It's okay to simply say, "You look great!" without making it about my "bravery." It's only bravery if you think I'm wearing something I shouldn't because I'm fat.

"Wow! You've gotten fatter!"

- Bodies change. That's common enough that I'm surprised you feel the need to comment on it.

- I get that you're surprised my body changed, but I'd really appreciate it if you didn't comment on it. Thanks.

"I would be miserable if I looked like you."

- I hope someday you'll love your body as much as I love mine.

- The anti-fatness in our society is vicious, and it's unfortunate you choose to participate in it.

"I can see your [points at your FUPA, or fat upper pubic area]."

- Are you trying to be helpful by pointing out that I am fat all over? Because I promise I am already aware of that.

- Yes. This is what my fat body looks like in workout clothing.

- If your intention is to shame me for this outfit, it's not going to work. I am wearing what I love and I am comfortable with my FUPA showing.

"Don't you know being that fat will kill you?"

- Are you trying to start a conversation about medical research and systemic bias toward fat bodies? Because there are other ways to open up that topic!

- I am not interested in your thoughts about my body or my health.
- There are a lot of things humans do that could kill us. Being fat isn't one of them.

"You'll never get a girlfriend if you don't lose some weight."

- Fat people date and have sex and enjoy relationships just like anyone else. It's not something I worry about.
- I appreciate your concern, but I'm getting plenty of action.

"I got you a gym membership for your birthday!"

- I think your intention is to be helpful, but by buying me a gym membership that I didn't ask for and am not going to use, you're wasting your money.
- Oh no! I wish you had checked with me first! That's not something I'm going to use, so I hope you're able to get a refund.

FOOD POLICING

"You don't need to eat that."

- Please don't comment on what I'm eating.
- Is there something wrong with the food?

"I brought celery sticks for you and cupcakes for everyone else."

- I wouldn't want anyone to feel awkward that I got celery and they didn't, so I'll have a cupcake too. But thanks for making a special effort for me!

- That's . . . odd. Are you trying to restrict what I'm eating when that's not something I ever asked you to do?

"Real men don't eat salad. They eat steak and potatoes!"

- Real men eat whatever *they* want and don't follow anybody else's silly food rules. I want a salad today.

- I'm pretty sure gender has nothing to do with salad or steak, but maybe you know something I don't know.

"[Your name] will take the leftovers home; they'll eat anything!"

- Thanks for thinking of me, but I don't want the leftover food.

- I know you're just joking, but the way you said that came across like fat shaming. Please don't make those types of comments about me.

"Maybe a bit of guilt and shame would make you think twice about what you're eating."

- Shaming me about what I eat won't stop me from eating, but it will stop me from eating around you. So if that's your intention, you've succeeded.

- It's okay for us to have different opinions about fatness and food, but it's not okay for you to make comments like that. Unless you knock it off, I'm going to leave now.

DIET CULTURE

"Are you on a diet?"

- I have a personal rule that I don't discuss diets while I'm eating. It tends to ruin the meal.

- I don't want to talk about diets today. Can we discuss something else?

"You should switch to being vegan!" "Have you tried keto?" "Maybe you could try intermittent fasting?"

- Unless I ask for a suggestion, please keep diet ideas to yourself.

- I get that your intention is to be helpful when you suggest I eat vegan/keto/fasting, but the impact of your comment is that I just never want to eat around you ever again.

- I'm excited for you that you found something that makes you so happy! When you bring it up like that, it sounds like you are judging me for not doing what you're doing. It's not something I'm interested in, but if that ever changes, I promise you'll be the first to know.

"I'm fasting today because I was bad last night and ate a whole plate of brownies!"

- Are you open to some feedback about what you just said? [They consent to receive feedback.] You're an adult and I respect your right as an adult to eat or not eat whatever you want. When you say you're starving yourself as a punishment for eating a treat, that is pretty alarming language! I have snacks in my bag I'd be happy to share so you don't go hungry all day.

- I feel really uncomfortable with the idea of restricting food as punishment. Do you need juice or crackers or something to tide you over?

FOOD ALLERGIES

"It has only a little peanut butter in it. I'm sure it's fine!"

- Nope! My peanut allergy includes all amounts of peanut products. That's not something I can eat.

- It's okay if you don't want to accommodate my allergy, but it's not okay to tell me that you will and then don't. I could've brought my own meal if you had told me you're only serving food with peanut butter in it.

"How was I supposed to know that her being 'allergic to corn' included corn syrup too?!"

- I know it was an accident, and you didn't feed her corn syrup on purpose. I'll send you a complete list of corn derivatives before she comes over here again.

- I think all of our emotions are a little heightened at this moment because a strong allergic reaction can be pretty scary to witness, but please don't raise your voice at me. If you need to step outside to compose yourself, I understand.

"You've got celiac disease, you're lactose intolerant, and you don't like vegetables? What do you even eat?!"

- Food! That isn't my favorite topic, so I'd appreciate it if we talk about something else. What shows or movies have you been watching lately?

- I know it sounds complicated because it is, so I'd like to take a break and not think about it right now. Thank you for understanding.

Grief & Trauma

Grief is like the ocean, and you're on the shore, looking over the waves. Sometimes the waves come crashing in big and full and heavy, you feel like you're drowning, and it lasts a long time! Sometimes the waves are small and lap at your feet, and you have a moment of missing, longing, wishing, and wanting.

Over time, there are fewer big waves, more small waves, and eventually fewer waves altogether. But you don't ever leave the beach. Part of you will probably always be there, and you can get hit with a wave of grief at any moment. A song, a smell, a memory, and *splash*! You've been soaked! It can feel like you're right back at the beginning of your grief again, as if you're being smothered by the first wave you ever felt.

If today you are drowning, the waves are tsunami-sized, and it feels like you won't ever come up for air, I get it. I promise the tide will change. I promise the waves won't hit this intensely forever. But I don't know how long it will be like this for you. My suggestion is to take each wave one at a time. Breathe between them as best you can.

Eventually, probably longer than you want but sooner than you think, the tide will turn, and the waves will shrink. I promise.

I combined grief and trauma into the same chapter because in my experience, they're related. Both are incredibly difficult with long lasting effects and can resurface like a sudden wave on the beach.

I've experienced both in my life, and it changes you. Here are several ignorant statements that I have heard while standing on the metaphorical shores of grief and trauma, and some suggested responses.

GRIEF

They press for details. "What happened? How did he die? Was it awful?"

- It's too painful for me to talk about any details today. Please respect my need for privacy.

- I'm not going to talk about this with you. Excuse me.

- I think you're trying to express care and concern, but it's coming across as morbid curiosity, and I am not going to answer any more questions about what happened.

- I think in general when someone is grieving, it's better to wait for them to share whatever details they're comfortable sharing instead of asking for specifics.

"You've been sad for too long."

- I think your intention is to encourage me to be happy, but what you just said came across as "I'm tired of your grief. There's something wrong with you that you're not over it yet." That really hurts.

- I read once that grief is love with no place to go. I will always love them, so I will always grieve for them.

- I understand if my sadness is hard to be around. It's hard to feel this sad all the time. It doesn't help to say that I need to stop being sad. There's not a switch that I can turn off.

- I think your intention was to be kind, but what I just heard you say was "I'm uncomfortable being around you when you're sad, and I want you to pretend to feel happier for my comfort." I'm sure that's not what you meant, but that is how it came across.

"She is in a better place."

- I know you meant that in a comforting way, but it doesn't feel comforting. It feels like you're saying you're glad they're dead.

- We have different spiritual and religious beliefs, so I disagree with that sentiment. In my opinion, there is no better place for them than here with me.

- I know that's something people say when they don't know what else to say because grief is awkward and intense. A better option is, "There are no good words for this."

"He wouldn't want you to still be sad. Cheer up!"

- Wow. I know you are trying to help, but that was not a helpful thing to say. A better option would be, "What can I do to support you today?"

- I know it can be uncomfortable to be around somebody who is experiencing really intense emotions for an extended period of time, but I don't think telling them to "cheer up" is the answer.

- If you need to excuse yourself, because this is too much, please do. But I will not pretend to be anything other than devastated right now.

- That's incredibly presumptuous to assume you knew him well enough to state he wouldn't want me to feel my feelings all the way through.

"At least they aren't suffering anymore!"

- I know you mean that in a comforting way, but it doesn't feel comforting right now.

- It's okay if you have reached your limit of listening to me talk about my grief, but it's not okay for you to try to limit my experience of grief by attempting to put a silver lining on this.

- In my experience, any sentence that starts with "at least" very rarely is as helpful or kind as intended. It feels like you're minimizing my grief.

- Instead of trying to cheer me up, which is impossible at this moment, will you please just sit next to me and hold my hand and feel sad alongside me? I don't need words. I just need you to be here with me.

"Everything happens for a reason."

- If believing in a cosmic conductor of events brings you comfort, I'm happy for you. But I personally don't like that expression, and I would appreciate it if you never said that to me again.

- That is not a helpful sentiment right now.

- I know you're saying that to try to help me feel better, but it comes across as "You're supposed to be in pain right now" or "You're being hurt on purpose," and both sound really cruel.

- I think your intention is to be comforting, but the idea that they died for some twisted, fated reason is the opposite of comforting at this moment.

TRAUMA

"Stop overreacting. It's not that bad."

- This is a proportionate reaction to what happened to me.

- Please consider if you are trying to minimize how awful it was because thinking about the extent of what happened to me is overwhelming to you.

- Are you asking me to suppress how upset I am because the intensity of my emotions is making you uncomfortable?

- What I'm hearing you say is that you are not a safe person to talk about this topic with.

"You're exaggerating."

- Why is it easier for you to believe I am exaggerating than for you to believe that something truly terrible occurred?

- You can choose not to believe me, but that doesn't change the truth of what happened.

- Actually, I'm downplaying a lot of details because I don't like reliving them. It was worse than I'm describing.

- I'm not an unreliable narrator, but you accusing me of that tells me you're an unreliable audience. I'm not going to talk to you about this anymore.

"What doesn't kill you makes you stronger!"

- I refuse to credit my trauma for my strength. I am strong, despite what happened to me, not because of it.

- I'm not interested in painting a silver lining on my trauma today.

- That's survivorship bias. Saying this awful thing made me stronger is ignoring all the people who didn't make it. That feels disrespectful to me.

- I know you have kind intentions in saying that, but I think that expression highlights a fundamental misunderstanding of how trauma affects people. I'm not strong because I survived trauma. I'm strong because after trauma, I had years of therapy, medication, and community care to heal from that damage. Imagine how much further along I could be if I hadn't needed to detour for a decade of recovery. What doesn't kill you still hurts for a long time.

"Other people have had it worse."

- You can drown in a puddle or you can drown in a lake. Either way, you drown.

- Are you trying to minimize what happened to me, or do you think comparing trauma is going to make me feel better?

- This is not the "Oppression Olympics." There's no prize for having the worst thing happen to you. It's all awful.

- I think your intention is to be comforting, but the way that came across was like "Stop hurting. You don't deserve to be upset about this. Your feelings are invalid." That is the opposite of comforting.

"Get over it! It happened a long time ago!"

- I promise if it was an option to just "get over it," I would've by now.

- Trauma literally changed my brain. There's no switch I can flip to get my previous brain shape back. Telling me to get over it is extremely unhelpful.

- I understand that my trauma triggers are inconvenient and probably uncomfortable for you. They're really hard to live with. If you want to have a conversation about boundaries so both of our needs can be met, I'm open to that.

- I get that you're frustrated, but it's not okay to talk to me like that. A better option would be saying, "I'm having a hard time understanding why this is still so intense for you even though it's been awhile. Can we talk about what you're experiencing right now?"

They joke about the word *triggered*.

- I get that the word *triggered* has taken on a broader cultural meaning in the last few years, but when I use it, I'm specifically referring to something really awful that is still affecting me. I would appreciate it if you wouldn't joke about "triggers" anymore.

- I hope you never find out for yourself what a trauma trigger actually feels like. It's not a joke to me.

- My brain automatically reacts to sensory stimuli that match what was happening when my trauma occurred. The same sights, sounds, smells, etc. It's an overwhelming sensation, and I wish you wouldn't joke about it.

- This is not a topic that I have a sense of humor about, so if the goal of your joking is to make me laugh, I suggest you move on to new material.

House & Home

I've worked as a professional cleaner in homes and hotels several times throughout my life. I learned that people all have different definitions of "clean" and are all sure their definition is "the right way." I also learned housekeeping is something the majority of people have no chill about. It must be cleaned a particular way or else it's completely wrong.

Even people who are unable to keep their homes the way they would like due to disability, lack of support, finances, or any other reason typically have an idea in their head of "the right way" to clean or what clean should look like.

I've encountered more shame with house care tasks in my 17 years working with clients than I have for anything else besides sex and bodies. It's as if our living space is an extension of ourselves, and we must keep it a certain way to be okay, which creates a multitude of issues when people with different ideas of "the right way" to keep a house occupy the same space!

Here are several statements and a scenarios to help you know what to say when someone inevitably judges that your way of cleaning isn't their "right" way.

"I would do the vacuuming, but you're just so much better at it!"

- It sounds like you need more practice!

- You are welcome to do all of the vacuuming from now on so you can learn to be as good at it as I am.

- Hmm. That sounds like strategic incompetence. That if you are bad at vacuuming, then you don't ever have to vacuum again because I'll do it. That's not something I want in our relationship.

- If you need help learning to vacuum, I'm sure there are wonderful tutorials on YouTube!

"I'm happy to help you clean up if you just tell me what to do!" [from a roommate or live-in partner]

- The idea that you are "helping me clean up" is casting me in the role of housekeeper boss and casting you in the role of housekeeper's assistant. I don't like those roles for us, so let's have a conversation about who is going to manage which chores in the house from start to finish.

- It really changes our dynamic from being equals to being dominant and submissive when I am the one always telling you what to do in the house. I didn't come into this relationship looking to be the dominant partner all the time, and I'm pretty sure you aren't hoping to be the submissive partner. Let's find another system that works for us as equals.

- Thank you so much for your willingness. You are a grown adult, and you do not need my permission to take responsibility for common household chores. Let's pull out our "Fair Play" chore cards and reconfigure who is in charge of what.

"My mother never let her house get this dirty."

- Your mom's house is not my house.

- Are you trying to start a conversation about the ways we were raised to clean by our caregivers, or are you trying to indirectly judge my housekeeping?

- I've personally never found it helpful to compare different people with different strengths and support needs and how they keep house. Do you find that comparison helpful for some reason I don't understand?

Your roommate or live-in partner puts dirty clothes on the floor next to the laundry hamper.

- Just a heads-up that I will be washing only clothing that is in the hamper from now on. If it's on the floor, you get to wash it yourself.

- When you leave your clothes on the floor next to the hamper, it comes across as, "I don't care that you have to do more work to pick up after me" or just "I don't care about you." Will you put the clothes in the hamper from now on?

- Hey, I've noticed lately you've been putting the clothes on the floor instead of in the hamper. What is going on?

"It's not that hard! All you have to do is pick up after yourself every day!"

- Just because it's easy for you doesn't mean it's easy for me. Not everyone has the same abilities and support.

- I know you're trying to be encouraging, but what you just said came across like "There's something wrong with you, and you should be deeply ashamed that your house doesn't meet my standards." If that's not what you meant, I would appreciate it if you clarified.

- Please don't offer me any advice about my housekeeping. If I have questions, I promise I'll ask you, but until I bring it up, I would rather we talk about anything else!

"Your house is kind of gross. Don't you ever clean?"

- I didn't invite you over to see my house; I invited you over to see me. If the house is preventing you from enjoying our visit, maybe we should reschedule for another time and place.

- I understand that you are trying to be helpful, but what you just said came across really shaming. It doesn't make me want to clean, but it does make me want to never let you through the front door again.

- Unless you're volunteering to clean my house, I would rather change the subject.

"I can't believe you've had dirty dishes in the sink for two whole weeks! What's the matter with you?"

- I shared that with you as a point of vulnerability, and you reacting in judgment is not helpful.

- Not that it's any of your business, but I have several health conditions that make dishes especially difficult to hand wash. Unless you're volunteering to wash them for me, it's really not your business.

- It's not morally superior to have all clean dishes over all dirty dishes. If I need those dishes at some point, I'll wash them!

"Have you ever heard of Marie Kondo? You would really benefit from her decluttering methods!"

- I appreciate that your intention is to be helpful, but unsolicited advice on how to declutter my home is not something I'm looking for right now.

- I'm practicing something called maximalism, where you try to have the most things you love in one space! It's awesome!

- I'm not interested in changing anything about my space. I like it the way it is. But if that ever changes, I will check out Marie Kondo's work. Thanks for the suggestion!

"Your house would look so much better with new couches and a coat of paint on the walls!"

- I think it's neat you always have a vision of how things can be better, but that's not a topic

I want to get into right now. Will you tell me more about your new job? How is that going?

- Unless you're volunteering to pay for those couches and paint the walls yourself, that's not happening anytime soon.

- I think your intention was to be supportive, but that came across more like "Your house looks terrible right now and you need to spend a bunch of money to make it acceptable to me." A better question would've been, "Is it fun for you to talk about decorating your space? If so, I'd love to have that conversation with you!"

They gave you cleaning supplies as a holiday or birthday present as a "hint" that your house isn't clean enough.

- Thank you for giving me something that I can tell you put a lot of thought into. I know your intention is to be helpful and kind, and I appreciate that.

- I'm not sure what your intention was, but giving me cleaning supplies that I didn't ask for feels more judgmental than helpful. Please don't do that again.

- If you're trying to hint that I should clean my house more, I promise I got the message. I'm not going to change anything about my housekeeping habits, but I am very clear now how you feel about it.

Hugs, Handshakes, & Touch

I'm a touchy-feely physical person who wants to cuddle, hug, hold hands, and be in skin-to-skin contact with the people I love! And many of the people I love are not huggers. They find touching other people sensorially overwhelming and would prefer we skip social handshakes all together.

I've learned to always, always, always ask before touching. "Hey, may I hug you?" "Would you prefer a high-five or a wave?" "May I sit next to you, or do you need space?" "Moving forward, are you okay with me kissing you without asking each time and then if it's not okay on a certain day, you'll say something? Or do you want me to keep checking in first?" "What amount of touch are you comfortable with right now?"

The person with the body is the boss. You are in charge of if, when, and how you want to be touched. My desire to cover my friends in physical affection doesn't override their desire to not be touched. Huggers don't get to pick when the hugs happen. Touch is an "everyone must give an enthusiastic yes or else it's a no" scenario. Here are some statements and scenarios to help you navigate setting boundaries with the touchy-feely physical people in your life.

HUGS

They open their arms for a hug, and you don't want to.

- I'm not in a hugging mood today. But I'd love a high-five!

- I'm going to skip the hug for now. Thanks anyway!

- No hugs for me; I'm limiting my close contact with people right now. It's so good to see you. How's everything been going?

"I'm a hugger. I hug everyone!" [then grabbing you for a hug]

- Oh no! I'm NOT a hugger. Please let me go. [Step back or away.]

- [Back up, turn, or put an arm out to stop them.] The last time I saw you, you hugged me even when I was visibly uncomfortable and then laughed it off as, "I hug everyone." I don't like hugs, and it's not okay for you to put your need to touch people over my need to not be touched. Don't do that again.

- [Step back with an arm out in a "stop" gesture.] I don't hug. I've told you that before. I'm willing to make this as awkward as necessary until you stop touching me when I've asked you not to.

"Don't be rude. Hug your grandma!"

- I'm the boss of my body, and I don't want to hug right now.

- Bodily autonomy trumps social conventions. If that's rude, then the social conventions need to change.

- Grandma knows I'm not trying to be rude. Sometimes I don't want to hug, and that's okay. It doesn't mean I don't love her.

"Come on now! Don't be unfriendly. Give me a hug!"

- Don't touch me. I'm willing to be as unfriendly as necessary until you back up and stop trying to hug me.

- I don't want a hug, and if that makes me "unfriendly," that's something I'm okay with.

- If you're trying to guilt me into hugging you, it's not working. Please respect my no.

HANDSHAKES

They offer their hand to shake, and you don't want to.

- I'm okay to skip the handshakes and just get right down to business.

- I don't shake hands for religious reasons, but it's good to see you. How was your drive over? Was there any traffic?

- I don't shake hands for health reasons, but I'm excited to be here. I have so many questions about the proposal you sent over. May I pull that up so we can get started?

They squeeze your hand too hard.

- Ouch! That hurt my hand. Please be more gentle.
- You might not be aware of how strong your grip strength is, but that really crushed my hand and it still hurts. Please be more mindful of your handshakes in the future.

"Don't be a limp fish! Put some power in that grip!"

- I have low grip strength because of a health condition. This is the only handshake I have.
- Please stop crushing my hand. It's painful.

"Your hands are clammy!"

- Yes, that happens sometimes. It's a sign I need to eat something.
- Oh! That's hard to notice on myself. Thank you for telling me so I can make sure I get my circulation up!

TOUCH

They touch you, and you don't want them to.

- Don't touch me.
- I need a lot more personal space than that. Please back up.
- I'm not a touchy-feely person. Please don't touch me without asking first.
- I startle really easily and being suddenly touched is the worst! Please don't ever do that again.

They poke or tap you to get your attention.

- I don't like being poked. Please say my name or wave your hand where I can see it if you need to get my attention.

- I know you're trying to be discreet by tapping me to get my attention, but I really don't enjoy it. Please just whisper my name or wait until later to tell me.

They rub your shoulders when standing behind you.

- Whoa. I don't like that. Please don't touch my shoulders!

- Yikes! Personal space! I'm not okay with being touched like that.

They put their hand on your lower back to move past you or guide you forward.

- Hands off! Please don't touch my back.

- I know you didn't mean anything by it, but I really don't like my back being touched like that. Please just say, "Excuse me" and wait for me to move out of your way.

Jokes & Humor

This chapter is all about what's funny and what's not funny, so let's start with a joke!

What do you call it when a British person takes a really good look at something?

Propaganda. (It sounds like "proper gander" in a posh London accent.)

I laughed so hard I practically fell off the bed when I first heard that! Silly word humor is my favorite.

I chose this joke for this chapter because humor and propaganda are closely tied right now in the news, on social media, and in groups promoting bigotry and prejudice. There's a clear pattern of using humor to normalize extreme viewpoints over time aka propaganda.

First, someone hears a joke that's subtly racist, sexist, transphobic, ableist, etc. and laughs. But if they get called out for enjoying something that doesn't seem like it's really hurting anyone, they'll probably feel shame and discomfort.

This shame and discomfort leads to them agreeing the next time they hear someone complain that "Everyone's too sensitive" or "We can't make any jokes anymore!" Because that matches what happened to them; they "got in trouble" for what was "just a joke"!

Instead of taking a step back and acknowledging they feel small for laughing at humor that "punches down" at a vulnerable person or group, often they seek to feel bigger by getting angry at the people who "get triggered over nothing."

It's a lot easier to refocus that internal discomfort into blaming someone else than to take responsibility for making a mistake. This leads them toward laughing at increasingly bigoted jokes and transferring any uncomfortable feelings that come up into anger at the vulnerable people who they claim are "making them feel this way."

The end result is their online activity and social groups are full of extreme views because that's who makes and laughs at "punching down" humor. They've been pulled through what I call the "humor-propaganda pipeline."

The way I can tell if someone is in the humor-propaganda pipeline is by how they react when I tell them a "punching down" joke isn't funny to me.

If they apologize and don't say anything like that again, they're not in the pipeline. They can accept feedback and make changes without blaming their temporary discomfort on me or the subjects of their "punching down" joke.

If they get defensive and start accusing me of being "triggered," "a snowflake," or that I'm "too sensitive," they're somewhere in the humor-propaganda pipeline. Most likely I won't be successful in changing their mind, so my best option is to set a boundary so they don't share that type of bigotry with me again.

That's what the statements and scenarios below are all about.

"It's just a joke!"

- I'm glad it's "just a joke" because then it won't be a big deal for you to never say it again.

- I'm glad because I would hate to think you really believe what you just said. It's pretty hurtful and seems out of character for you.

- Okay. But I'm not joking about disengaging with stuff like that. Please drop it.

"You're being too sensitive."

- I'd much rather be sensitive than insensitive.

- My sensitivity is one of my favorite things about myself.

- I don't think it's possible to be "too sensitive" about hate speech and bigotry. That's something I'm glad to be sensitive about.

"Get a sense of humor!"

- You're right that I don't have a sense of humor about hate speech.

- Different people have different senses of humor, and mine does not include laughing at vulnerable people.

- There are so many other things we could be laughing about right now. I don't understand why you're insisting on making jokes that I already told you aren't funny to me.

"Why do you take everything so seriously?"

- I love to laugh, and I'm happy to laugh when something is funny. Bigotry isn't funny to me.

- Am I "taking everything so seriously," or are you shifting blame onto me for your discomfort that I called you out?

- This is serious to me, because the people you were joking about are people that I know and care for. I would take it just as seriously if someone was making cruel jokes about you.

"Well, I think it's funny."

- I know it's uncomfortable when you get called out. I've been called out too a few times, and I don't like that feeling. I hope you know I told you it's not funny to make jokes about vulnerable people because I believe you're better than that. I think you're a genuinely funny person. You can find other stuff to make people laugh that doesn't rely on punching down.

- Jokes rely on a shared understanding, and I don't understand why you think making mean comments is funny.

- One of the things I really like about you is that you are so funny! I think you have the skill and ability to make people laugh without relying on prejudice stereotypes for an easy punchline.

"You're such a buzzkill."

- I can tell that you're feeling defensive, and I know that's uncomfortable for you. Calling me names is not going to help the situation.

- I know it's uncomfortable when we're just joking around and then somebody makes it really serious and calls you out for saying something inappropriate. I'd like to just get back to having fun, and the fastest way for that to happen is for you to apologize for being insensitive, and then we can all move on.

- I want to laugh with you, and it would be easier to do if you were making jokes that I think are funny instead of saying mean things about people. If that makes me a "buzzkill," okay.

When they "punch down" at people with less power than them.

- Your joke is kicking at people when they're already down, and it's not funny to me.

- Please don't make jokes about marginalized people around me.

- I'm not okay with making fun of vulnerable people just for a laugh. Please don't say stuff like that.

"You can't say anything anymore!"

- You can say whatever you want, but so can I. And I'm saying the joke you made is not funny to me.

- You're right that we've entered an era of accountability. You can still say whatever you want, but you're a lot more likely to be called out if you say something offensive.

- I think as the world becomes increasingly connected, our general awareness of vulnerable groups has increased. Like once there might've been a single gay person in your local neighborhood, but now there's a massive connected gay community online, so if you say something anti-gay, there's a lot more people who will react to that. That leads to an increase of accountability.

"Everything's too politically correct these days!"

- I think "political correctness" is just compassion in fancy language. And I'm really okay with more compassion in the world.

- Is it "politically correct," or is it just caring about people? Because I know you absolutely care about people! That's the kind of person you are. I'm a little surprised that you would object to an opportunity to express more care for people.

- Look. You're a wonderful person, and if I didn't think you were a wonderful person, I probably wouldn't have taken the time and energy to let you know that what you said was offensive. I would've just let you go on your merry way, continuing to offend people thinking that you're being funny. But because I care about you, I gave you some feedback that what you said was not okay. Now, you have the opportunity to either accept that feedback or ignore everything I said and blame it on "political correctness." That's up to you.

"Stop being such a snowflake."

- I know you mean that as an insult, but I actually really love snowflakes, so I'm okay with you calling me that!

- When you say that, what I'm hearing is "I don't want to take responsibility for making an inappropriate joke, so I'm going to blame you for my discomfort right now."

- Maybe the person melting down when asked to stop making inappropriate jokes should be called the "snowflake"?

Money

When I was 13 years old, I babysat the neighbor's six children for a couple of hours and she paid me $20. And when my mom came to pick me up, she took the $20 out of my hand and handed it back to the neighbor lady and said, "Oh, you don't need to pay her."

I was so furious! It's one thing if I had known from the beginning I was babysitting for free to support a neighbor in need, but to expect payment and then get it taken away? Not okay.

Years later as an adult, I was married, I had a house, I had a yard, and I did not have time to cut the grass. I saw the 14-year-old neighbor boy starting up his lawn mower, so I went out to ask, "Hey, you're out cutting your grass this afternoon. Can I pay you to also cut mine?" He did a wonderful job and even edged by the sidewalks, which was more than I was expecting!

Then about an hour later, there was a knock on my door, and it was him and his dad. His dad had taken the money from his son and handed it back to me to say, "Hey, you don't need to pay him."

At that moment, I got justice for 13-year-old Kami!

I took the money and handed it back to the boy (not to the dad) and said, "He deserves to get paid."

By communicating clearly and setting this boundary, I became who I needed as a child.

Below are some statements and scenarios to help you say the thing about money.

"May I borrow some money?"

- No.
- I'm not in a position to lend you any money.
- I don't lend money. I only give it. I'd be happy to give you some money, and if you get a chance to give it back someday, that's great! But it's also okay if you don't. I'd never want money to be an issue between us.
- Yes. Let's have a conversation about a repayment schedule and write out a contract we will both sign so it's really clear what the plan is.

"Stop being so cheap; you're embarrassing me!"

- My intention is not to embarrass you. My intention is to get a good deal. I would rather talk about this in private.
- Would you prefer to handle the transaction since this matters to you so much?
- I like being cheap! It's kind of a rush to get the best deal on something. I understand that you're uncomfortable right now; what can we do so we both get what we want?

"We're family! I can't believe you don't want to help your family! I paid for everything your whole life, and now I need help and you won't loan me a dime? What's wrong with you?"

- I already said no, and I'm not going to change my mind. Please stop asking me.

- I can tell you're probably pretty scared that you won't be able to get the money you need. I'd like to have a conversation about what all the options are, but I'm not going to do that if you continue to shame and blame me for not immediately saying yes to your request.

- I think it's reasonable for me to ask questions about what's going on before loaning you a large sum of money. If that's not something you're comfortable with, I understand. I'm not comfortable giving you a loan without more information.

- You are legally obligated to provide for any biological children. That doesn't entitle you to your children's money when they become adults. Trying to guilt me into loaning you money is not going to work.

"How much money do you make?"

- Why do you ask?

- I have a personal rule that I don't discuss money while trying to enjoy myself; it tends to ruin the mood.

- Are you trying to start a conversation about income disparity or the gender pay gap or something?

"How much is your rent?"

- Are you trying to find out average rent prices in this area?

- More than it should be!

- Pretty standard for this area; why do you ask?

"How much did your house cost?"

- I'm happy with what I paid for it.

- Is this a roundabout way of determining if I make more or less money than you?

- I'm pretty sure you can look it up on Zillow or something if you really want to know.

"Wow. I bet that was expensive!"

- It's true I paid more for higher quality, but it tends to last longer.

- Yes! And worth every penny!

- I think "expensive" is relative. Like what's expensive for one person might be standard for another.

Responding to people panhandling or busking.

- No.

- I don't have anything for you today.

- Unfortunately, I can't.

- I don't have any cash on me, but I'll be coming back this way in about 45 minutes with lunch. Can I pick you up something from the taco place?

"I'm not going to give him money! He'll just spend it on drugs!"

- Humans love what makes us feel better. Almost every adult I know uses something to make themselves feel better, whether it's sugar, caffeine, nicotine, alcohol, adrenaline high, or anything else! The difference is some people get to do that in the privacy of their own homes, and some people do not. I invite you to expand your perspective a little.

- I'm pretty sure if you were stuck sleeping outside, you would want something to make yourself feel better or warm you up too!

- You get to do whatever you want with your money, but I think your judgment of how he would use that money is really off base.

"You're acting like a gold digger."

- If you have a concern about my choices, I'm willing to discuss that with you. But please don't call me names.

- I think your intention is to express concern, but the way that came across sounds like "You're selling yourself for money, and I'm judging you to be a lesser person because of it." Is that what you meant?

- You don't have to like how I make a living, but it's not okay to make derogatory comments about me. Please don't say that again.

"I bet she's just with him for his money."

- I tend to think other people's relationships are not my business, unless they specifically asked me for my opinion.

- We're not on the inside of their dynamic, so there's no way of knowing what their reasons truly are, and I think it's unkind to speculate.

- I don't think you meant it to come across this way, but that's a really gross, sexist thing to say. What if we just stuck with, "I hope they are really happy together!"

Names & Pronouns

I've legally changed my name twice in my life. I've had a maiden name, a married name, and now my chosen name: Kami Orange. Because of my own experience finding power and joy in picking a name that makes me happy every time I write it anywhere, I feel fiercely about names!

I'm an advocate for calling people by their correct names, a.k.a. the names they have chosen for themselves to be called, which might not be their government paperwork names. I practice using the right pronunciation of someone's name. I am careful to spell it the way they spell it. Names are really important to get right because it communicates, "You matter to me."

I've never changed my she/her pronouns, but I've got a lot of loved ones who have. If pronoun changes are not something that are part of your daily life like mine, it might be difficult to understand why using correct pronouns is such a Big Deal. It's like with names. Using someone's correct, chosen, preferred, picked-out-for-themselves pronouns says, "I see you. You matter to me. Your identity is valid. I support you in being your true self."

Here are some scenarios and statements to support you in responding when people call you or those around you by an incorrect name or pronoun.

NAMES

They use an incorrect name.

- My correct name is [correct name].

- Oh! I changed my name. It's [correct name] now.

- You mean [correct name]! She recently changed her name.

- Just a heads-up, his name is [correct name] now. I can give you the spelling if you want to update your phone contact info.

- My name is not up for debate. I changed it and will only be answering to [correct name] from now on. Please use my correct name.

- I don't want to make any assumptions, so I'm just going to ask you directly. It's been several weeks since I changed my name, and you keep calling me by an incorrect one. Are you trying to be hurtful, or is something else going on?

- I know you have good intentions when you apologize over and over after messing up my name. But when you do that, it makes it all about you and your feelings. When it's *my* name. Please just say a quick "oops! I meant [correct name]" and move forward.

- It's been several weeks since I changed my name. Your persistence in calling me by my incorrect name is starting to come across as discriminatory. If that's not your intention, please do some practicing on your own time to get my name right from now on.

They mispronounce your name.

- My name is pronounced [correct pronunciation].

- Oh! My name is actually pronounced [correct pronunciation]. The emphasis is on the second syllable.

- I've told you twice already that my name is pronounced [correct pronunciation]. Would you please take some time on your own to practice so we can stop having this conversation? Thank you.

- Your persistence in saying my name wrong is starting to come across as discriminatory. I've corrected you multiple times, telling you that my name is [correct pronunciation] with the emphasis on the second syllable. What needs to happen for you to get this?

"But why did you change your name?"

- Because I wanted to!

- Because I like my new name more than my old name.

- I wanted a name that reflects who I am now as a person.

- It's incredibly common for people to change their names at significant life transitions. Bobby grows up to be Robert. Prince became The Artist Formerly Known as Prince. My grandma changed her last name when she got married. Your resistance to me changing my name comes across as you having a problem with me, not about my name itself.

"Why didn't you change your name when you got married?"

- I didn't want to.

- I like my name more than their name.

- Are you trying to start a debate about my name? Because that's not something I'm going to argue with you.

- I always wonder why people rarely ask husbands why they didn't change their names. Why does it have to be the wife who is expected to go through the legal and social hassle of changing their name?

"Isn't that a boy's name?"

- It can be a masculine or feminine name. What matters is that it's my name, and I love it!

- Nope! I'm a woman, and it's my name. I was named after my grandpa, and I love my name for the family history involved.

"But what about your parents? They gave you that name!"

- A name is a gift, and once a gift is given, it belongs to me to do what I want with it. I'm grateful for the name my parents gifted me; it was a good name for a while. Now I have a new name.

- It's really odd that you're claiming to "respect my parents" by using my birth name instead of my currently correct name. Your behavior is the opposite of respectful, and if my parents were here, they would tell you that.

PRONOUNS

They use the incorrect pronouns in reference to you or someone else.

- My correct pronouns are she/her.

- Oh! They changed their pronouns. They're using "they/them" now.

- I'm not debating his correct pronouns with you. Please use he/him from now on.

- I've asked you to use my correct pronouns multiple times now, and you keep persisting in using the wrong ones. What is going on?

- I get that changing pronouns for someone is probably a new experience for you. At this point, it's been [number] weeks and your persistence in using my incorrect pronouns is coming across as discriminatory.

- Moving forward, I am not going to respond to incorrect pronouns.

- You have the choice to practice my correct pronouns on your own time. You have the choice to access the myriad of free resources online to help you learn my correct pronouns. You have the choice to quickly correct yourself when you make a mistake. And I have the choice to avoid you if you use the incorrect pronouns to refer to me.

- Your choices are to use my correct pronouns when speaking to me or to not speak to me at all.

"It's too hard for me to change your pronouns. I'm old!"

- When you say "it's too hard to change pronouns for me," it comes across as "I don't care about you enough to practice."

- You can decide that you're not willing to learn something new or you can accept that it might take you a bit of extra practice, but being "old" isn't an excuse for using someone's incorrect pronouns.

- That's because over 40 years ago we lost almost an entire generation of LGBTQ people to the AIDS epidemic. Culturally, we are decades behind in how we use and understand gender-affirming pronouns. Otherwise you wouldn't think being "old" is an excuse for using incorrect pronouns.

- It might take you more practice, but it is really important to me that you use my correct pronouns.

"I just don't get the whole pronoun thing."

- Are you genuinely asking so you can learn something new, or are you "just asking" to disguise intolerance?

- You don't have to "get it" to respect it and use the correct pronouns for someone.

- Pronouns might not be a big deal to you, but they are a big deal to me. Even if you don't understand why, I would appreciate if you made an effort to use my correct pronouns.

- Would you correct yourself if you misgendered a dog? Then I think it's okay to be expected to correct yourself when you misgender a person.

"I care too much about grammar to call you 'they.' 'They' is plural, not singular."

- Claiming you can't use someone's correct pronouns because of a grammar rule comes across as you care more about rules than people. Is that what you're trying to say?

- The simplified version of grammar you were taught as a child might not have included singular they/them pronouns, but they have existed and been used for over 600 years.

- You keep saying that you're "the grammar police" so you can't stomach the fact that people use singular they/them pronouns. Language changes, and I would think that "the grammar police" would want to be on the cutting edge of linguistic innovation.

- This is something you can easily google if what you really care about are the correct grammar rules for singular they/them pronouns. I suggest the *Merriam-Webster* dictionary, which will tell you singular they/them predates the 1300s.

"Neo pronouns aren't real. You're just making stuff up!"

- I'm not debating the validity of ze/zir/zirs and other neo pronouns with you.

- Just because you don't know about something doesn't mean it's not real. That's not how the world works.

"I don't have pronouns; I'm just normal!"

- I don't know if you are being intentionally offensive or unfortunately ignorant, but everyone has pronouns.

- You might not know what your pronouns are, but that doesn't mean you don't have any.

Politics

I live in the United States of America, where having intense debates about political issues has become the norm. It feels like politics are everywhere, all the time. But not every situation is suitable for a discussion about who deserves care in our society and how that care should be allocated, such as when you're with coworkers who have vastly different political views than you, or when you're traveling in a car for the next several hours with someone, and they bring up a divisive topic.

Even when I know the person I'm talking to is not going to change their mind, I refuse to normalize prejudicial beliefs by staying silent and allowing them to think I agree with them. How much I explain depends on the situation and the audience.

If it's one-on-one, I usually state that I don't agree with what they just said and then change the subject.

If it's a group setting, I usually state that I don't agree with what was said, explain briefly why I don't agree, and then change the topic. The explanation of "why" is so anyone listening will understand why it wasn't okay for me.

In my experience, people who start a conversation about politics by bluntly stating an offensive belief like it's a fact usually aren't open to changing their minds.

I refuse to debate politics with closed-minded individuals because neither of us are going to change our views. I choose to use my energy to connect with people who are open to new viewpoints, which is why I share a brief explanation of the reasons I disagree when there's an open audience. The audience often will change its mind based on what I said, and I feel like that's a good use of my energy.

It's important to also consider safety when speaking up about politics—or anything you or others feel strongly about. If it's not safe for me to speak up, even to disagree, I feel no guilt for not doing so. Safety first!

Included in this chapter are some general statements about politics and scripts to help you disagree in a kind and direct way.

They bring up a politically divisive topic in a setting where you don't want to get in a disagreement.

- Can we talk about this later please? I'd rather not get in a heated debate right now.

- We see that very differently, so let's move on to another topic.

- If you're sharing that with me because you are assuming that I agree with you, I don't.

- I'm pretty sure neither of us are going to change our minds tonight, so let's just focus on [this nice dinner/completing this sale/celebrating the bride/etc.] instead.

- That's not a topic that I am willing to discuss right now.

"It's not polite to talk politics at the dinner table."

- It's okay to say you don't want anyone to talk politics at your dinner table. It's your house and your rules. But that doesn't mean politics are inherently impolite to discuss.

- I think your intention is to say you want to have a nice dinner and only speak about calm topics, but the way you phrased that came across as shaming me for disagreeing with a bigoted statement. You didn't speak up when they made that political "joke," but you did when I took offense to it. Why is the burden of politeness on me but not on them?

"I don't care about politics. It doesn't affect me."

- Wow. That is the opposite of how I feel. I care deeply about politics because they affect me and people I love every single day.

- You might not have the time, energy, or interest to care about politics, but that doesn't mean politics don't affect you.

"I don't vote; it doesn't make a difference."

- You're right that there's a lot more to creating social change than just voting, but I also think it's quite privileged that you have the option to vote and choose not to when so many people have fought for you to have that right at all.

- That's your right. Personally, I always vote because I'm incredibly suspicious of anybody telling me that my voice doesn't matter. It makes me wonder who benefits from the narrative that voting doesn't make a difference. Possibly people heavily invested in the status quo?

"All political parties are basically the same."

- If you're interested in having a substantial discussion on this topic and are open to changing your mind, I'd be happy to talk to you about it. Otherwise, we should change the subject, because I really disagree with what you just said.

- Are you trying to start a debate about politics right now? That's not something I'm interested in doing today.

"Why do you make everything so political?"

- Life is political. Unless you have enough money to buy a government, politics affect everything in your life.

- It's okay to say that you don't want to talk about politics anymore today or you've reached your limit for heavy topics. It's not okay to imply there's something wrong with me being passionate about the politics that affect my daily life and those I love.

"Why do we have to pick sides? Why can't we all just get along?"

- As the human rights activist Desmond Tutu said, "If you are neutral in situations of injustice, you have chosen the side of the oppressor."

- When one side wants to just exist peacefully and the other side doesn't want the first side to exist at all, it's not possible to "just get along."

"Freedom of speech! You can't tell me not to say that!"

- Freedom of speech doesn't mean freedom from consequences. I can absolutely say I won't tolerate that type of talk around me and that I will think you're awful and limit how often I'm around you if you keep sharing those offensive beliefs.

- You can say whatever you want, but I can choose not to engage with it. I'm leaving now.

- If you sincerely believe my objection to you saying something offensive is an oppression of your rights, that "freedom of speech" applies only to you but not to me, then I'm not interested in continuing this conversation.

Racism

I'm a white woman from a 92-percent white community in Utah, United States. I have a lot of personal and client experience teaching white people how to respond to racists. I have minimal personal and client experience supporting people of color (the global majority) because of the demographics of where I live and work.

What I know about antiracism I learned from Ijeoma Oluo, who defined racism as "any prejudice against someone because of their race, when those views are reinforced by systems of power." I have also learned from the works of Maya Angelou, Reni Eddo-Lodge, Sabrina Strings, Imani Barbarin, and Mona Eltahawy; also the stories of Henrietta Lacks, Michael Brown, George Floyd, Breonna Taylor, and so many more Black, Indigenous, and people of color activists, writers, creators, and educators.

If you are interested in learning more about antiracism, I encourage you to seek out the works and stories of the people I've listed above for more in-depth responses to racism. If you are a person of color, you are the expert on your own experiences. The below statements are meant as a guide for responding to overarching racist comments, and I acknowledge it's beyond my expertise to suggest responses to more specific comments.

Included in this chapter are several exclusionary statements that I've heard used to separate people of the global majority from white people.

DENIAL

"I'm not a racist. I have a Black friend!"

- That's not how that works. If you're open to learning something new about racism it sounds like you may not know, I'd be happy to send you a link to a video about this.

- Having a Black friend doesn't exempt you from racist systems where people with white-sounding names are hired over people with Black-sounding names or where Black people don't receive pain medication when white people do for the exact same symptoms.

- I think we're defining "racist" differently. To me, there are two types of racism: individual dislike of someone because of their race, and systems of power hurting people because of their race. So it's possible to be a racist because you're participating in those systems that hurt people even if you personally don't dislike people of a certain race.

- I didn't think I was racist either until I learned more about racism! Turns out that having friends of the global majority isn't related at all to socially benefiting from my whiteness. Like I accidentally walked out of the hardware store with an item on the bottom of my cart that I didn't pay for, and it was no big deal to go back in and return it. But my Black friend gets followed through the store to make sure she's not stealing anything, and if she accidentally took something without paying, the store would call the police or ban her from shopping there again! That's racism.

- I can tell you're feeling defensive that you got checked for saying something racist. I get that. It can be uncomfortable when we realize we've accidentally said or done something that hurts people. Now you know that [describe words or actions] is a thing racist people do so you won't do it again!

"I don't care if they're white, black, red, yellow, purple, or polka dot! I don't see color!"

- Oh! I think what you meant and what you just said don't match. The expression "I don't see color" means "It makes me uncomfortable to think about how society treats certain people because of their race so I prefer to ignore it." I think what you're trying to say is "I want every race of people to be treated equally."

- Hmm. May I offer you some feedback on what you just said, because I don't think what you meant is what's coming across in your word choice? [They consent to receiving feedback.] In saying "I don't see color," you're accidentally denying someone's racial identity instead of protesting the racial oppression that I know you're against.

- I think your intention is to be inclusive by saying "I don't see color." I get that! I appreciate that you're not okay with people being treated differently because of their race. In my experience, the phrase "I don't see color" often comes across as you're not willing to acknowledge the systems of racism that do "see color" and make it harder for certain people in society. A better phrase would be "I support all people, especially those being judged unfairly for the color of their skin."

- "I don't see color" can come across as "I won't believe you when you share your experiences of systemic racism" or "A large part of your identity is not important to me."

- When you say "polka dot" as an example of race, I know you're trying to lighten up a heavy topic. Personally, I don't find that funny because it feels like you're minimizing the real effects of systemic racism on people of the global majority. Will you please not say that around me again? Thanks.

MICROAGGRESSIONS

"Where are you really from?"

- Are you asking what my ethnicity is? Like if I've ever taken a DNA test? Have you? Which DNA test did you take?

- I know you meant that in a curious-getting-to-know-you type of way, but it came across in a "your skin is brown so you must not be from around here" type of way. A better question would be, "I'm born and raised in [city name]; what about you?" So you share where you're from first and then people can answer it however they feel comfortable.

- Why do you ask?

- My understanding is everyone is made of stardust. Like our bodies are composed of the same elements as stars. So I guess I come from the stars!

"Oops! All you people look alike."

- Please don't say "All you people look alike." The "you people" part is especially offensive and comes across in a racist way that I know you aren't intending. It's best to just apologize and move on with the conversation.

- Hey! It's not okay to say that. Just because you're unfamiliar with how a particular ethnic group looks doesn't mean they all look alike.

- I get that you're uncomfortable that you mixed up Nikau and Rua again because they're both Māori, but it's not okay to say "All you people look alike." A better option is "Rua, I'm sorry I mixed you up with Nikau" and then move on with the conversation and do your best to not mix them up again.

- May I offer you some feedback on what you just said? [They consent to receiving feedback.] When you say, "All you people look alike," it sounds like you're saying "I can't be bothered to learn about you or identify you as an individual." That's really unkind and doesn't match who I know you are as a person. In the future, try keeping it about your struggle and not blame a whole group that you can't tell people apart. Maybe you could say, "My brain doesn't differentiate people very easily, so I'll probably mix you up with someone else, and I hope you can forgive me."

"Your name is too hard to pronounce. Do you have an English name I can use instead?"

- No. My name might be unfamiliar to you, but it's *my name*. I'm not changing it because you're unwilling to practice a few times on your own to get it right.

- I know you meant it in a "let's find a solution" type of way, but the question "Do you have an English name?" comes across as "I want everyone to adapt to what's convenient for me because I'm not willing to make an effort to adapt to others." A better option would be, "Will you help me with the pronunciation of your name? I want to get it right."

- Hmm. I don't think you meant to come across in an "English-speaking people are the most important" type of way, but that's how that question sounds. I'm happy to help you with the phonetic pronunciation of my name, but I'm not changing it. This is my name.

- Oh, no. I'm named after my grandmother, and I would never dishonor her memory by making up an "English name," especially considering the history of colonization in her country.

- What you just said came across like, "You are too weird and foreign; you should change yourself to fit in." One of the things I've always admired about you is how much you value individuality and self-expression, so I know you didn't mean it that way because that's not who you are. Maybe a better question in the future would be, "I love your name! Will you help me pronounce it correctly?"

RACIST "COMPLIMENTS"

"You speak really good English."

- Thank you. So do you. Is it your first language? It's my third.

- I know you meant that as a compliment, but it comes across as "I wasn't expecting someone who looks like you to speak English like I do" and feels really othering. Would you have said, "You speak really good English" to someone who is white?

- When you told Charna that she "speaks really good English," I don't think it came across as the compliment you were intending. Maybe you didn't realize this, but she's a local, so she speaks English.

- How would you feel if someone seemed surprised that you spoke "really good English"? It would be weird, right? Because you've been speaking English all your life. That's how I'm feeling right now.

- Well, my ancestors were colonized by the English just like yours were, so I grew up speaking English.

"You're so articulate."

- Oh, why do you say that?

- What does that mean to you? "Articulate"?

- Oh! I know you meant that in a kind way, so I'm going to let you know that's a common thing racist people say to mean, "I'm surprised you are capable of speaking on the same level as me. I assumed you wouldn't be as smart or educated because of the color of your skin." A better option is to use a specific example when you're complimenting someone like, "I loved how you outlined the pros and cons of the Matthews decision. That level of clarity was really helpful."

- I appreciate the compliment and because I wouldn't want anyone to ever misconstrue your good intentions, you need to know that the phrase, "You're so articulate" is a common thing racist people say when they're surprised a person of color is smart, so I get that it's a compliment, but it's probably not a compliment that you want to keep repeating.

- Hmm. May I offer you some feedback on something it sounds like you don't know yet? [They consent to receiving feedback.] When you told Kareem that he's "so articulate," it accidentally came across like you were shocked a Black man could speak eloquently on a complex topic. Like, "Wow! You're as smart as a white man!" I'm sure that's not how you meant it *at all*. A better compliment strategy in the future is to be specific about the content of what he's saying instead of overall how he's saying it.

"I bet you're really good at math."

- Are you saying that because I'm Korean? You know that's a racial stereotype that's not true about all Asians, right?

- China ranks first in the world in math, but it also ranks first in reading, and as far as I know nobody's going around saying "I bet you're really good at reading because you're Chinese."

- Thank you. I know you meant that in a kind way, so I want to give you a heads-up that "You're really good at math" is something racist people often say to Asian people as a stereotype. A better option would be, "I admire your problem-solving skills" or "Thank you for helping me figure that out!"

- I know you had good intentions when you told Misaki that she's probably really good at math and then asked her to calculate the tip for lunch, but I wanted you to know that it came across as "You must be a human calculator because your family is from Japan." Another way to say that would've been, "Would you like to calculate the tip or should I?" and left her ethnicity out of it completely.

- It's okay to tell someone you admire their problem-solving skills, but it's not okay to link it to their race. It contributes to the "model minority myth" and is harmful toward Asian people.

OVERT RACISM

"She only got into the program to meet a diversity quota."

- Wow. That's a really offensive accusation toward both Zuri and the program selection committee! Please don't ever say that again.

- I'm not trying to start a debate, but I need to let you know that's what a racist person would say, so I am really shocked that you would repeat something like that.

- I don't think that's the case, because she's extremely talented and qualified to be here.

- That's not okay to say, and I think you're missing the whole point of the program. People with the same backgrounds tend to solve problems in the same ways. The more diversity in the program, the more unique the approaches to problem solving.

- If you want to have a discussion about the intricacies of affirmative action and diversity quotas, we can, but it sounds more like you're saying Shanti's only qualification to join the program is her race, which is both an offensive thing to claim and completely untrue.

"They're taking our jobs."

- If you want to have a sincere discussion about how immigration improves the economy, we can! But if you're only interested in blaming other people for your financial struggles, then we should talk about something else.

- It sounds like you're really scared that your job skills won't be enough to support your family and you're looking for someone to blame. Personally, I blame the billionaires hoarding astronomical amounts of wealth and not my hardworking neighbors who are trying to put food on the table just like we are.

- I'm really surprised to hear you say that! I know how much you value family and hard work, so I would've assumed you admire people who sacrifice so much to provide for their loved ones.

- If by "they" you mean billionaires, then yes. They are taking our jobs by outsourcing to countries where it's easier to exploit people. It's really gross.

- If by "they" you mean people of color and by "our" you mean white people, that's a pretty racist way to say, "I'm worried about being able to support my family in this economy, and I'm looking for someone to blame."

"Those immigrants are ruining this country."

- Wow. That's both untrue and really unkind. I'm surprised to hear you say something like that. You're typically very welcoming to everyone.

- Unless you're Indigenous and your family has been here for 30,000 years, I'm pretty sure you're an immigrant. And from that perspective, it's our family's immigration that ruined this country!

- What I'm hearing you say is that you're scared about how things are changing and you've been told to blame other people who are trying to provide for their families, just like you. Dividing people by race so they don't organize by class and demand better is a really effective strategy to keep the poor poor and the rich rich. I think you're smart enough to see through that manipulation and blame the people who are really ruining this country: billionaires.

- Hmm. I think people in power keep repeating that because if they can get you to blame immigrants for the problems that have existed in this country for a long time, then they don't have to take responsibility for fixing anything.

- I'm not sure if you meant that in a racist way, but that's definitely how it came across. Please don't ever say that to me again.

"All lives matter!"

- Wow! I'm really surprised you would say something like that. Maybe you're not aware that's an expression that people use to say "Black lives don't matter." I know that's not what you mean, so I encourage you to not use that expression again!

- If you're open to having a sincere discussion on the over-policing of certain groups, I'd be happy to talk to you about it. But if you're just going to repeat racist catchphrases, I'm not interested in continuing this discussion.

- I think when you use that expression, you're trying to say you believe everyone deserves to be safe and have their needs met. But unfortunately it's coming across as "white people are the most important" because of the origins of that phrase.

- I think it's kind of suspicious that expression only came about after activists rallied to stop the over-policing of Black people in America. So whether or not you meant it in a "I think everybody deserves to be safe" type of way, it sounds more like "I don't care about Black people."

Recreational Substances

I was raised by religious parents who believed the only stimulant we needed was a relationship with God. No caffeine, alcohol, or smoking. I didn't even know what cannabis was until my friend got her car stolen when we were 19 years old. After it was found abandoned and got returned to her, I commented on the funky smell. She said, "That's weed."

"What? What type of weeds?" I asked. I thought she meant someone had hauled garden weeds in the back seat of her car and it left a smell.

"No, weed, like the drug." she replied. "They smoked weed in my car."

I've come a long way since that innocent misunderstanding and have now experienced most legal recreational substances at least once. My viewpoint is that adults can choose to use legal substances like caffeine, alcohol, nicotine, cannabis, and psychedelics for pleasure or medicine if they want to.*

This chapter includes examples of judgmental statements about recreational substances and ways you can respond.

Please note that cannabis and psychedelics are not currently legal in all jurisdictions, and many legal substances are still limited to those age 21 or older in the United States.

CAFFEINE

"Can't live without your coffee, huh?"

- You've commented on my morning coffee a lot, and I think your intention is to just make conversation, but it's starting to come across as judgmental. In the future, I would appreciate it if you commented on the weather or traffic instead.

- You have made several comments lately about how much coffee I drink. Are you expressing concern about my caffeine intake or just trying to make conversation?

"I don't put poison in my body."

- It's okay for you to choose not to consume caffeine. It's not okay for you to make snarky comments about my caffeine. Please stop.

- I'm not interested in debating this with you and would appreciate it if you didn't comment again about what I am drinking.

"I don't need coffee like you do because I get enough sleep at night."

- I'm glad you found something that works for you. This is what works for me. Let's talk about something else.

- Are you actually talking about yourself right now, or are you pretending to talk about yourself to make a judgment on how much coffee I'm drinking? Because I'll celebrate anyone getting a good night's rest, but

I'm not interested in discussing my coffee habits with you.

"I get a natural high from the gym, so I don't need caffeine. Maybe you should try it."

- I know health is something you're passionate about, but please don't give me any advice about my body unless I specifically ask you to.

- I understand your intention is to be helpful by making suggestions of how I can change my habits. Unfortunately it's coming across in a "I'm judging your choices because I'm better than you" type of way, which I'm sure isn't what you want. Please wait until I directly ask you before giving me any health improvement ideas.

"Wow. Another energy drink today?"

- I do what works for me!

- You've made several comments lately about the caffeine I drink. I think your intention is to express concern for my health, but it's coming across in a "shame on you" type of way. Please don't mention my energy drinks again unless I bring it up first.

NICOTINE

"Smoking is so gross."

- Telling me that smoking is gross or that I'm gross for smoking won't make me stop smoking, but it will make me avoid you. Unless that was your goal, please don't comment on my smoking habits again.

- When you say, "Smoking is so gross" because I'm getting up to go outside and smoke, all it does is make me stay out there longer and need to smoke more to calm down because I feel anxious being in here with you judging me. If you really want me to stop smoking, we can talk about that. But just telling me I'm gross isn't the answer.

"Kissing you is like licking an ashtray."

- If your intention in saying that was to encourage me to never kiss you again, then you have succeeded.
- It's okay to ask me to brush my teeth, use mouthwash, or chew gum before kissing you. It's not okay to compare my affectionate gesture to my partner with "licking an ashtray." That hurts my feelings, and honestly, I now want to avoid ever kissing you again.

"Vaping is bad for you."

- Unless I'm specifically asking you for health advice, please don't give me any.
- When you say that, I think your intention is to express concern for my health. Unfortunately it comes across as "I'm judging you" or even "I'm better than you." A better option is to ask me, "Are you open to having a conversation about the health effects of vaping?" And wait for me to say yes to talking about it with you.

"Why can't you quit?"

- It's not helpful to ask "Why can't you quit?" like it's a simple matter of willpower. What we call "willpower" is really just dopamine regulation, and some brains are more genetically efficient at dopamine regulation than others. I'm doing the best I can with the brain, the resources, and the support I have.

- When you ask questions like that, it doesn't help me stop smoking, but it does make me want to avoid you. Being alone is the opposite of what people trying to quit smoking need. The most helpful thing you can do to support me is distract me from needing another cigarette.

"You know that's bad for you, right?"

- Shaming me for my choices doesn't make me stop making those choices; it just encourages me to hide those choices from you. If that's your intention, then you have succeeded.

- Are you really asking me if I know that or are you trying to dissuade me from smoking?

ALCOHOL

"You don't have to be totally sober; just don't go crazy!"

- You and I drink different amounts, and if you have a sincere concern about how much alcohol I drink, I'm open to talking about that. But telling me that I am "going crazy" is not the way to start that conversation.

- I drink alcohol in a safe and responsible way. I'm not clear where your judgment that I am "going crazy" is coming from.

"Do you have a drinking problem?"

- Why do you ask?
- The way you said that sounds kind of judgmental, so I hope I'm misunderstanding you and you're asking out of genuine concern for my health.

"You kind of seem like an alcoholic."

- To me, an alcoholic is someone who drinks every day or binges out of control. I think having a few drinks in a social setting is normal.
- You're right that I drink more than you do, but that doesn't make me an alcoholic. Are you trying to start a conversation out of sincere concern for my health?

"He can't hold his liquor, can he?"

- What does it mean when you say that? Do you think he's in danger, are you implying he's weak, or what?
- Are you suggesting we cut him off and send him home for the night?

CANNABIS

"Stoner!"

- Oh! Maybe you don't know this, but "stoner" is a term of affection within the cannabis community, but it's not really an appropriate thing to call someone if you're not in that community.

- Do you think everyone who uses cannabis is a stoner? Is that what you're trying to say?

"Why do you think you need that?"

- Why do you wear glasses? They're a tool to help you function and navigate life easier. That's why I use cannabis. It allows me to function in my daily life.

- Considering it was prescribed by my doctor, you'd have to ask her!

"Your house stinks."

- Are you saying you need to step outside because you have a fragrance sensitivity, or are you judging that we smoke?

- It's okay to leave if you don't like the way my home smells, but it's not okay to criticize the me on your way out.

"I can't believe you get high every day!"

- I think you're conflating recreational cannabis used for fun and medicinal cannabis used for function. They're not the same thing. I use cannabis every day to function.

- I understand how that might be shocking if your only experience of cannabis was getting high for fun at a party or something. Since I'm using it medicinally, I do need it every day.

"Oh sure, it's 'medicinal.' Right."

- If you're open to learning more about medicinal cannabis use, I'd be happy to send you some information. Otherwise, we should change the subject because it's obvious we don't see eye to eye on this.

- I'm not okay with being judged for following the plan created by my health professionals. You don't have to understand to be respectful.

- If you continue being judgmental, I'm going to have to ask you to leave.

PSYCHEDELICS

"I thought you were more careful than that."

- I am careful to only use psychedelics in a safe and responsible way.

- If you're interested in learning about all of the ways I'm careful with my psychedelic use, I'm happy to share that with you. But I'm not okay with being judged for something you don't have all the information on.

"I don't understand why you would engage in such risky behavior."

- Are you trying to start a conversation about safe psychedelic use because you're curious? Because a better question would be, "Psychedelics are new to me. Will you explain how you mitigate the risks involved?"

- It sounds like you're unfamiliar with the vast amount of scientific research being done on the benefits of psychedelics. Do you want me to send you some information, or should we switch the topic and talk about something else?

"Why would you ever even consider trying it?"

- If you really want to learn, I'm happy to share my experience with you, but I'm not interested in being judged for what is both a spiritual and medicinal aspect of my life.

- I didn't get it either the first time I had a friend share with me about their psychedelic experience. But I was intrigued and decided to work with a psychedelic therapist and ultimately had a profoundly transformative positive experience.

"I don't trust you anymore now that I know you do drugs."

- I will always support you in doing what you feel is best for you. I'd like the opportunity to explain how psychedelics for therapeutic purposes are vastly different from street drugs for recreational purposes, but I understand if that's not a conversation you're comfortable having right now.

- I'm not sure if you're imagining me meeting sketchy characters in a back alley somewhere, but did you know there's multiple clinical trials happening right now for using psychedelics with PTSD patients or in couples therapy? I think your distrust is based on some old information.

"That's not safe."

- I appreciate that you care so much about my safety and if you want me to go through all the ways I'm ensuring I use psychedelics in a safe, responsible manner, I can walk you through it.

- Is there anything I can say that would help you feel better, or is this a topic we just need to agree to disagree on?

Relationships

Relationships are complex and ever-evolving yet wonderful and life-affirming! I've had many types of relationships in my life.

There were times I had only acquaintances for a while but no true friends, a close friend group, friend breakups, favorite people, a best friend, and currently I'm in a large circle of amazing platonic connections that I love to serve and nurture.

I've been single, married, divorced, monogamous, non-monogamous, platonically nesting partnered, in open relationships, in closed relationships, and am currently sexually, romantically, and domestically partnered with my lover, referred to in this book as Sexy Beast.

The point is: it changes. Whatever is happening with your relationships—whether sexual, romantic, domestic, or platonic—I hope the below statements in this chapter help you best communicate your situation.

RELATIONSHIP STATUS

"Why are you still single?"

- I know you're just trying to make conversation, but it's getting kind of old that you ask me that every time I see you. Better questions would be, "How are things going with your new podcast?" or "Have you been to any good restaurants lately?"

- I'd appreciate it if you'd take an interest in what is happening in my life beyond my relationship status. If there's ever an update in the relationship department, I'll let you know.

"Are they 'the one'?"

- I'm glad you're so excited for me and my relationship. If things move forward, I'll let you know. But until then, I'd appreciate it if you didn't ask for status updates.

- Asking if someone is "the one" feels like a lot of pressure that I'm not interested in accepting. What I can tell you is that they are wonderful, and I am happy.

"When are you moving in together?"

- If it happens, I'll let you know. Until then, I'd rather you ask about how work is going, or what's new with Charlie and Claude?

- I appreciate that you're so eager to send us a housewarming gift, but please stop asking when it's happening until I give you an address of where to ship it. Thank you.

"When are you getting married?"

- I love how much you love love. Remind me, what year did you get married? Will you tell me about your wedding?

- Thank you for caring so much about me that you really want to see me be married. You ask for an update every time we talk, and because I don't have any updates, I'm starting to dread our conversations. It would mean a lot to me if you would stop mentioning marriage until I bring it up. Is that something that you can do?

"Aren't you lonely by yourself?"

- I know you're asking out of concern, but that question really sounds like "I think there's something wrong with you that you don't have a partner right now." If you're worried about me being lonely, you can invite me to lunch or text me funny memes more often.

- Are you trying to start a sincere conversation about my mental health, or are you just making dinner party small talk? Because while I appreciate the first, I'm only in a headspace for the second.

"Why did you break up/separate/get divorced?"

- Why do you ask?

- I don't talk about my breakups when I'm out having fun. It tends to ruin the mood.

MONOGAMY

"You're going to get bored being with just one person forever."

- I don't think the opportunity to witness someone's life, from the big things like having kids and cross-country moves to the little things like how they hum when they're really happy, is ever going to be boring to me.

- I get that monogamy isn't for you, but please don't tell me how I'll feel in the future. I know what makes me happy.

- Apparently you don't know me as well as you think, or else you wouldn't say that.

"Don't ever go to bed angry!"

- Being tired makes everything seem much more dramatic than it actually is. A good night's sleep almost always fixes the issue.

- I've found that arguing late at night never works out well, so we actually always go to bed angry and usually wake up to realize it wasn't worth fussing over at all!

- In my experience, people who say that aren't night owls, so their "going to bed" is like 9 P.M., and there's still time to talk it out before it gets too late. I'm a night owl, and there are no productive sorting-things-out conversations at 3 A.M. at our house.

"You have to buy flowers or jewelry to make her happy." "You have to keep the house clean and look pretty to make him happy." "You have to have sex all the time to make them happy."

- Thank you for telling me what's worked for you in your relationships. I'm going to keep doing what's working for me, but if it ever stops, I know who to ask for advice!

- I don't subscribe to the idea that there are one-size-fits-all solutions to relationships. I get that these strategies worked for you, but I'm going to do what I feel is best for my relationship.

- That doesn't match my experience, but thank you for sharing.

"If you really loved me, I wouldn't have to tell you what I want."

- I wish being in love gave me mind reading superpowers, but unfortunately I will only know what you want if you tell me out loud with words.

- I can tell you're feeling some pretty strong emotions about this. Are you in a place to problem solve right now, or do you need me to just listen to you talk first?

- What I'm hearing you say is you're not feeling like your needs are being met and you wish I could do what would make you feel better right now without having to ask. Is that what you meant?

NON-MONOGAMY & POLYAMORY

"You must have commitment issues."

- I think having more than one partner is the opposite of "commitment issues" because I'm committed to multiple people.

- Are you asking out of genuine concern for my happiness and well-being, or are you simply judging something you don't understand?

"It's still cheating no matter what you call it."

- Cheating means people are sneaking around and hiding their partners from each other. In polyamory, everybody is aware of everybody else; there's no sneaking or hiding.

- It sounds like cheating is the only form of non-monogamy that you're familiar with. There's also swinging, open relationships, spouse swapping, throuples, polyamory, and more. Cheating is unethical and nonconsensual. Everything else I just listed is ethical non-monogamy, because everyone is a consenting adult who has agreed to non-monogamous relationships.

"You obviously don't really love your husband if you're sleeping with someone else!"

- I understand that if you love monogamously, then loving polyamorously is a totally unfamiliar concept, but that doesn't make it okay for you to accuse me of not loving my husband. That's a really unkind thing to say and completely untrue.

- Just because you wouldn't be able to sleep with someone else when you are really in love with your husband doesn't mean that's how it works for *me*.

"Oh, so you're greedy? You'll sleep with anybody."

- If this is you asking me if I'll have sex with you, it's not going very well. Is that the point that you were trying to make?

- No. Polyamorous doesn't mean promiscuous. That's a misconception. I'm really selective about my partners.

- Yes! I'm absolutely greedy for sex! It's part of my hedonistic values. However, that was true before I was non-monogamous. Most non-monogamous people are as particular or even more so in choosing their play partners as monogamous people.

"There's no way an 'open marriage' could ever work."

- It's okay if you don't want an open marriage. You definitely don't need to choose that. But it's not cool to judge other people's marriages when it's not something you have any experience with.

- I get that this is new for you and there's a lot you want to ask me, but I've been doing this for years, and honestly I've already passed my limit of answering newbie questions. There are some great books and podcasts that I'm happy to recommend for you if you're really interested in understanding how open marriages work.

"She can be with other women because that doesn't really count, but I'm the only man she can be with."

- That's pretty sexist and not respectful toward her bisexuality. I hope you're really clear with any potential partners about what your dynamic is.

- Thank you for telling me. That's not something I'm comfortable being part of.

- I find it gross when you say women-loving-women relationships "don't really count." Would you reconsider being so biphobic?

FRIENDSHIP

"Men and women can't just be friends."

- I don't subscribe to 70-year-old gender norms. It's possible to be emotionally close with someone without sleeping with them.

- I think the idea that two adults can't interact platonically without being overcome by a sexual compulsion is really strange. There are more intimacies in life beyond just sexual.

"So are you really 'just friends'?"

- The way you asked that makes me think you're worried there is something romantic happening between [friend's name] and me. You are important to me, and if there's something I can do to reassure you, I'd like to know what that is. Because I am "just friends" with [name].

- Yes. You seem really concerned about the details of my friendship with [friend's name]. Why is this so important to you?

"You don't have a best friend? Why not?"

- There are many types of friendship: work friends, neighbors you wave to and cat-sit for each other, college roommates, online connections, list-them-as-your-emergency-contact close friends, etc. I'm not interested in choosing one friend above any other.

- I'm really happy and fulfilled with the quality and quantity of friendships I have.

"You have to be loyal to your friends, no matter what!"

- I respect that is what works for you. That's not something that I believe. I'm okay that my friendships will ebb and flow as my life changes and evolves.

- It's a normal part of life that sometimes friendships will end. I'm not going to set myself on fire to keep other people warm.

Religion & Spirituality

There are over 4,000 religions, denominations, and faith groups in the world, plus thousands more individual spiritual practices and traditions. That's way more than I could cover in one chapter, so I focused here on the top misconceptions and prejudiced statements I've personally heard. As a practicing pagan who believes in a sentient Universe, I was raised as a Christian extremist and now live in a predominantly Mormon-Christian community, so I run into misconceptions about religion more often than not.

RESPECT

They don't respect other people's religious practices.

- Please don't make fun of other people's religious traditions.

- Just because it's unfamiliar to you doesn't mean it's okay to call their beliefs "weird."

- I get that you're curious, but you're asking me lots of questions that are starting to feel a little invasive. I would prefer you to look this up online if you really want to know more.

- You don't have to believe it to respect it.

They push religion in non-religious settings like work, school, etc.

- I prefer to keep my spirituality private and not discuss it at work.

- I think it's great that you have something you believe in so strongly. Please trust that I also have something I strongly believe in, and I'm not interested in changing that.

- That's not a topic I want to get into right now.

- I appreciate your curiosity, but I'm not going to answer questions about my religion while I'm at work. Thank you for respecting my privacy.

- Thank you for caring about my soul. I've got it taken care of, but if that ever changes, I know you're available. Unless I ask for help, please respect my privacy on this topic.

They pray out loud before a meeting begins at work or school.

- Instead of a group prayer, can we opt for a moment of nondenominational silence?

- When you opened the meeting with a prayer yesterday, I was really caught off guard. I didn't object at the time because I didn't know what to say, but I wanted to let you know that I'm not okay with a group prayer before we start working.

- I'm not comfortable combining religion and work/school. What do I need to do to opt out of this?

- Even if everyone here is the same religion, I still don't think it's appropriate to open our meetings with a prayer. I feel strongly that each person should be able to voluntarily opt into religious activities instead of being forced to either participate or opt out at work.

They assume you are part of their religion.

- Not everyone believes what you believe.

- I think you're making a reference to something specific to your religious practices that I am not familiar with.

- Oops! I'm actually not part of your religion, and I don't know what you're talking about.

- Based on what you just said to me, it sounds like you're assuming we believe the same things, but we don't.

- I get that you're trying to relate what I believe · to what you already know, but that's a really Christian-centric [or other religion] way to ask and it's kind of insensitive. A better question would be [example].

"My religion says that's not okay, so you shouldn't do that."

- I'm going to choose to follow my religion instead of yours, and my religion says it's a commandment, so I am going to do it.

- I don't practice your religion, so I'm going to do what I want.

- You're welcome to believe and do whatever you want, and I'm going to believe and do whatever I want.

- I'm not part of your religion, so I don't need to follow those rules.

PAGANISM

"You're culturally appropriating Indigenous traditions."

- You're right that some pagans use practices, tools, and terminology that they have taken from Indigenous traditions. There are also pagans who have been invited to participate in certain ceremonies and traditions. The only way to know is to ask that individual pagan where they learned what they are practicing.

- Are you referring to shamans and shamanic rites? Because there are lots of traditions worldwide that have spiritual leaders referred to as shamans.

"Do you sacrifice animals and dance naked under the full moon?"

- The way you phrased that sounds pretty judgmental, but I'm going to answer you anyway. No to the first and sometimes yes to the second.

- There are a lot of myths and misconceptions about pagans. Why do you ask? Are you looking for an invitation to our next ritual?

CHRISTIANITY

"You're anti-science."

- There are Christians who are anti-science, and there are Christians who are pro-science and everything in between.

- Are my personal beliefs surrounding science impacting you in some way I'm not aware of? Do you have a specific concern?

"You believe women should be subservient to men."

- There are some people who use religion to oppress women, but that's not something I personally practice or believe in.

- Why would you say that? Are you trying to start a debate? Because that's not something I'm interested in right now.

"You hate LGBTQ people."

- Unconditional love doesn't mean unconditional agreement. I can love someone without agreeing with everything they do.

- Actually, I'm part of a congregation that welcomes and supports LGBTQ people. I'd be happy to answer any questions if you're interested.

ISLAM

"He looks like a terrorist. I don't want to sit by him."

- Whoa! You don't have to sit anywhere you don't want to, but it is not okay to call someone a terrorist because they're Muslim.

- That's both ignorant and Islamophobic. Don't say anything like that around me again.

- If we're going to go around judging how dangerous someone is based on how they look, there's a lot of people in here dressed like rapists, serial killers, and mass shooters, and I'm not talking about the Muslim man in a turban.

"Is someone forcing you to wear a hijab?"

- I know you're asking because you care about me, but that's both an ignorant and offensive question. A better option would be asking, "May I ask you some questions about your hijab? I'm curious about why you wear it."

- It's really not any of your business. Whether or not someone wears a hijab is between them and God.

- I get that you're just curious and didn't mean for it to come across this way, but there's a lot of offensive assumptions about me, my family, and my religion in how you asked that question.

"Can I see your hair? I won't tell anyone if you take your headscarf off."

- No. The only people allowed to see my hair know better than to ask that question.

- From how you asked that, it sounds like you have a fundamental misunderstanding of how hijab works. I am absolutely not taking my headscarf off for you.

- If I wanted you to see my hair, I wouldn't be wearing a headscarf right now. Please don't ever ask me that again.

HINDUISM

"You're Hindu? That's the yoga religion, right?"

- There's a lot more to the world's oldest religion but, yes, yoga is a part of Hinduism.

- It's more accurate to say that's the majority religion of India because it's much bigger than just yoga. If you're curious, I encourage you to look Hinduism up online to learn more.

"Do you worship cows?"

- No. I believe all life is sacred, including cows, but that doesn't mean I worship them.

- We honor and adore cows, but we don't worship cows like we worship the Deity. The cow gives more than she takes, so by honoring her we honor all forms of life.

They judge you for eating meat because they assume you're vegetarian or judge you for being vegetarian because they think you should eat meat.

- Not all Hindus are vegetarians as part of belief in ahimsa, the principle of nonviolence.

- I think how people practice their religion is very personal, and it isn't something I want to discuss right now.

- I get that you have opinions and feelings about eating meat. So do I. Since talking about it is unlikely to change either of our food choices, let's move on to another topic.

BUDDHISM

"Do you think you'll get reincarnated as a bug?"

- Are you trying to start a sincere conversation about my beliefs, or are you making a joke that I am not understanding?

- Nope! It's a common misconception that all Buddhists believe in reincarnation.

"Is Buddha like your Jesus?"

- If you're asking if they were both spiritual teachers who emphasized compassion, yes. If you're asking if the Buddha is my god, no. There's a lot of great resources online if this is something you want more information about.

- I understand you're just trying to learn and relate what I believe to something you're already familiar with, but a better non-Christian-centric question would be, "Will you tell me about the Buddha?"

"You have to meditate every day and wear robes to be a Buddhist."

- It seems like you have a lot of questions about my beliefs. This isn't something I want to discuss at school, but I'm happy to recommend some books if you want to keep learning on your own.

- Nope! That's a myth. Buddhist leaders will wear robes, but most Buddhists dress like the everyday people that they are!

JUDAISM

"Hanukkah is like Jewish Christmas, right?"

- Nope! It's a minor holiday. Our big annual holiday is Passover in the spring.

- Nope! Totally different. Just because they both happen in December doesn't mean they're the same.

- I know you're asking because you just want to learn and are trying to avoid offending anyone, so I need to let you know that comparing Jewish traditions with Christian traditions is not okay. There's a long history of oppression, so a better approach is asking, "Will you tell me about your Hanukkah traditions?"

They start speaking Yiddish around you after finding out you're Jewish.

- Are you using Yiddish words like *schlep* and *mensch* around me because I'm Jewish? Because that's not necessary.

- If you're using Yiddish words on purpose to help me feel included, I appreciate the effort, but it's having the opposite effect because I know it's not how you usually speak. It's like you think you have to change how you are because I'm Jewish. Please stop.

- It's one thing if you start using Yiddish words after spending time around me and you pick them up just from hearing me say them, but it's another thing if you immediately start using them right after you find out I am Jewish. What is going on?

They make an anti-Semitic slur or comment.

- That's not an okay thing to say. Please don't ever repeat that around me again.

- I'm going to give you the benefit of the doubt that you weren't aware that what you just said is anti-Semitic. It's really offensive toward Jews, and it's best if you never say that again.

- That's a lie about Jewish people that has been repeated for decades, and it's really offensive. Don't talk like that around me.

- What you just said is something people in hate groups say. I'm shocked that you would repeat that because that is not the type of person you are, unless there's a side to you that I was previously unaware of. Why would you say something so awful?

ATHEISM

"You're not a good person. You don't believe in anything!"

- I don't accept that. Different people believe differently and that's okay.

- If you're trying to start a conversation about my beliefs, or lack thereof, this is not the right way to go about it. A better option would be asking, "Will you tell me about your decision to be an atheist?"

"You're going to hell."

- Considering that I don't believe hell exists, that would be quite the surprise!

- If you're trying to insult me, it's not working. If you're trying to express concern, it's also not working. A better option would be saying, "I really care about you and am concerned about what will happen to your soul in the next life. Can we talk about that for a bit?"

Sex

I love embracing my sexuality, whether it's learning the science behind human sexuality, reading spicy alien romance novels, or practicing with my partner(s). One of my favorite things about sex is how unique it is to each person but also how incredibly similar what humans think is arousing. It's fascinating!

I didn't grow up in a sex-positive or even sex-educated family. I remember being 19 years old, cuddling fully clothed on a couch while watching a movie with a young man. He said, "You're so sexy. You really turn me on!"

"How can you tell?" I asked.

"Can't you feel it?" he replied in a seductive voice and pushed his pelvis against the side of my thigh. I must have had a clueless look on my face because he paused and said in a regular voice, "You do know how men get turned on, right?"

Nope! So we paused our movie and had an impromptu sex education lesson about the lump in his jeans. Thank you to that guy for being so kind to explain something I had never learned until that moment.

Now I'm the person who gets phone calls and texts from friends asking obscure sex questions. I've taught sex classes, helped couples, given private coaching demonstrations, written erotica, and so much more! The statements in this chapter are organized into the three categories I use to define sex: self sex, partner sex, and multi-partner sex. Enjoy!

SELF SEX

"You masturbate? But you're a woman!"

- Self sex is awesome for adults of all genders if that's what they like.

- Over 40 percent of women have self sex at least once a month. It's a really normal thing to do.

"It's weird that you own a bunch of sex toys."

- I think it's weird that you don't own a bunch of sex toys. Why would you not want tools to improve your self sex experience?

- Just because something is unfamiliar to you doesn't mean it's weird. There's no reason to shame me for seeking pleasure.

"It's not okay to get yourself off if you've got a partner."

- It's okay if that's what you choose to do, but that's not something I believe in. Self sex is totally different from partnered sex. I like both!

- I am responsible for my own sexual pleasure and satisfaction. There's no pressure on my partner for our sex to be a certain way if I'm making sure my own needs are met. Having self sex allows me to relax and explore partnered sex more!

PARTNER SEX

"I'm not going to use a condom. I don't like the way they feel."

- If you want to do any type of penetration tonight, then condoms are non-negotiable. If you'd prefer no condoms, we can do hands and toys instead!

- If condoms are a no-go for you, then the options I'm comfortable with are we either wait to have sex until you find a condom brand that fits you better or we wait to have sex until we both get STI tested [and decide on another type of birth control (if applicable)]. What would you prefer to do?

"Do you have anything I should know about?"

- Are you asking when was the last time I got an STI test? Two months ago. I was tested for chlamydia, gonorrhea, syphilis, and herpes. What about you? When was your last STI test and what were you tested for? How many partners have you had since then?

- Yes. I have HSV, herpes simplex virus. I'm not having an outbreak right now and haven't for months, and I have been taking my meds for it, so the likelihood it's contagious is extremely small but not zero. The best option is to use condoms and dental dams.

- Yes. I'm HIV positive. I am consistent with my antiretroviral meds, and my viral load is undetectable, so it's not contagious.

"You probably want the lights off, huh?"

- Are you asking if I don't want the overhead light shining in my eyes, or are you asking if I'm uncomfortable with you seeing my fully naked body?

- The way you phrased that question came across in a body shaming way, like, "I'm assuming you want to hide what you look like during sex." Was that your intention?

MULTI-PARTNER SEX

"Aren't you worried about diseases?"

- Are you asking because you care or are you asking because you're judging?

- If you're trying to start a conversation about how people having multi-partner sex coordinate things like STI tests and birth control, a better option is asking, "That's something I would like to try with my partner. May I ask you some questions about the nitty-gritty details?"

"What if someone gets jealous?"

- It's okay to feel jealous. It's what you choose to do with that jealous emotion that determines if everybody is having a good time or the evening ends in tears.

- Multi-partner sex isn't for everyone because not everyone wants to navigate the potential emotions, including jealousy, that might come up. That's okay. If someone gets jealous, we talk it out.

"You want a threesome? Am I not enough for you?"

- Okay, let's back up. You asked me what sexual fantasies I have that we have never tried. I shared that I've thought about threesomes with the understanding that we're talking pie-in-the-sky ideas and not let's-put-this-on-the-calendar-next-week plans. Before we ever involved someone else in our sex play, we would have conversations about how we're each feeling and only proceed if we both feel good about it.

- I think threesomes are a "three yeses or it's a no" deal. If not everybody is enthusiastically saying yes, then we're not doing it.

DURING SEX

"Why can't you get it up? Are you not attracted to me?"

- It's a common misconception that erections are only about being physically attracted to someone. There are lots of other factors like stress levels, medications, sleep, health conditions, refractory periods, and more. I am very attracted to you, and I'd love to do other sexy things in the meantime!

- I can tell from how you asked that that you are feeling stressed about what my lack of erection in this moment means about how I feel about you. Sometimes it doesn't happen. Bodies are weird. That doesn't mean I'm not interested in you!

"You're better at this than I thought you'd be!"

- I'm not sure you meant it this way, but that was definitely a backhanded compliment, like you're saying "I was anticipating you wouldn't be very good in bed, and you surprised me." A better option would've been saying, "I'm really enjoying this with you!"

- I am not a fan of how you phrased that. Will you say it a different way?

"I'm not going to go down on you. That's disgusting."

- It's okay if you don't want to have oral sex with me. It's not okay to say that my body is disgusting.

- Whoa. You don't ever have to do any sex stuff you don't want to do, but do not say going down on someone is disgusting. Just because it's not your thing doesn't make it bad.

"Why don't you shave or trim your pubic hair?"

- My body hair is how I like it. I don't shave or trim it because I don't want to.

- You're getting the privilege of seeing me naked, and that privilege will be revoked if you keep making comments like that.

"Oh, you're into that? You're one of those freaks, aren't you?"

- Are you seriously kink shaming me right now? That's going to end our sexy times real fast.

- It's okay if that's not something you want to try, but it's not okay to try to shame me or call me names for liking certain things.

SEX WORK

"Sex work isn't real work and should be illegal."

- Are you trying to start a debate? Because it's not working. Unlike sex work, which *is* real work.

- One of the things I've always admired about you is that you care a lot about vulnerable people, so I'm assuming you are against legal sex work because you've been told that will help keep people safe. My understanding is that keeping sex work illegal allows bad people to take advantage of sex workers because they can't go to the authorities for help without facing charges. To me, legalizing sex work actually better aligns with your values.

"I wouldn't ever date someone who is a sex worker. That's gross."

- You do get to set your criteria of who you will date, but you don't get to speak badly about sex workers in front of me.

- Sex workers aren't "gross." Don't say stuff like that around me again.

"I bet you can't get laid unless you pay for it!"

- I support sex workers, and I'm happy to pay them for their labor if I ever use their services.

- I know you're just joking, but what you just said perpetuates harmful stereotypes about sex workers. Please don't say that around me.

Sexism

When I was 9 years old, my elementary school teacher told our class, "I need some big strong boys to help carry these chairs!"

I was so confused, thinking to myself, "I'm the third tallest kid in our class. I can swing on the monkey bars all the way across, so I have strong arms. Why did the teacher ask for only boys? I'm going to help anyway!"

I walked over and started moving chairs. My teacher stopped me and said, "You can sit down, Kami. I asked for only the boys to help. These chairs are heavy."

The division by gender instead of ability didn't make sense to me then, and it doesn't make sense to me now! If you ask a mixed group of adults to carry chairs based on who can easily lift 40 pounds, you'd get a mixed response. There might be a man with a back injury who can't lift anything, and there might be a woman powerlifter who can carry 440 pounds!

The weird cultural gender divide shows up in a variety of sexist ways, and these next statements are just a few examples.

WOMEN

"Well, we know what time of the month it is!"

- Bringing up menstruation because I told you something you didn't want to hear is sexist. Don't do that again.

- Making a "joke" that implies my mood today is connected to whether or not I am menstruating is discriminatory and not funny.

"Stop being hysterical."

- Having normal human emotions in an unexpectedly high-pressure situation is not "being hysterical." If you're trying to help, you could say, "What can I do to support you right now?"

- I know you have good intentions, but the term *hysterical* has a heavily misogynistic history. Hysteria was thought by the ancient Greeks to be a medical condition where a woman's uterus wandered through her body and made her act irrationally. It's not an okay thing to say when someone is upset.

"She's crazy."

- She is having a proportionate response to what's happening. That's not crazy; that's completely sane.

- You're attempting a debate strategy called ad hominem where you can't successfully disagree with what she said so instead you're attacking her character. It's not going to work.

"She's such a bitch."

- Have you ever noticed that if we call a man "a bitch," that means he's weak, and if we call a woman "a bitch" that means we disagree with her?

- You can just say, "I disagree" without the sexist name calling.

"Calm down."

- I appreciate that you're trying to help, but nothing is wrong. You are misreading me, and I don't need to be talked down.

- Would you ask a man to calm down right now, or would you celebrate how passionate and driven he is?

"I think you're in the wrong room; this is the meeting for managers."

- Are you assuming I'm not a manager because I'm a woman? Because that's how that came across. I really hope you have another explanation besides blatant sexism for why you just said that.

- I am a manager. I hope you take this as a learning moment and don't ever make a sexist comment like that again.

Refers to women as "girls."

- When you call adult women "girls," it's sexist and infantilizing. Please don't do that again. It's a habit worth breaking!

- Would you call the men on the programming team "the programming boys"? No. So please don't call the women on the programming team "the programming girls."

"I want to see the doctor, not the nurse." [Assuming you, the doctor, is a nurse because you are a woman.]

- We have amazing nurses here, but I'm actually Doctor [your name]. What seems to be the issue?

- You must have some pretty strong sexist expectations to assume the person standing in front of you with a white coat and a "Doctor [your name]" name tag is a nurse.

MEN

"Grow a pair!"

- I don't like that expression. Will you say, "Buck up" instead? Thanks.

- I appreciate you trying to encourage me, but I'm uncomfortable with the sexism implied by "grow a pair," like only people with testicles have courage. Will you say, "Just do it" or "You got this" instead?

"Don't be a pu**y."

- I know you mean "Don't be weak" when you say that, but all I'm hearing is you don't have a lot of respect for people with vulvas.

- That's a sexist slur. Please don't use that expression around me.

"Don't be weak."

- Courageously expressing your emotions is a sign of strength, not weakness.

- It's really sad that you got told "Don't be weak" when you were struggling and needed support so now you repeat it to others when they're struggling because you don't know any other way to support them.

"Real men don't cry."

- It's okay to say it's not the best time or place to cry, but it's not okay to shame someone for crying. Humans cry. It's totally normal.

- Crying is a physiological tool that releases endorphins in my brain to regulate stress. I think using all the tools available is the most "real man" thing I could possibly do.

"Don't be a little girl about it."

- You obviously don't know very many little girls because they are fierce and dangerous forces of nature! I wish I was more like a little girl.

- How do you think your daughter would feel to hear you say that being like her is an insult?

"The old ball and chain won't let you, huh?"

- It's weird you'd assume I'm a prisoner and my wife is my jailer. We don't play like that, but if that's your kink, have at it!

- My partner and I are a team of equals, not a boss and subordinate. I know you meant it as a joke, but please don't talk about us like that again.

"I can tell who wears the pants in your family!"

- I said I need to check with my girlfriend before committing to that, so you made a "joke" about my lack of manliness? I'm really surprised you'd say that. I know you're someone who respects your partners, so why would you imply respecting my relationship is something I should be ashamed of?

- Everyone wears pants in our family. Unless we're wearing leggings, which have a better range of motion!

"Boys will be boys!"

- I know you're saying that in a funny way, but I really don't like that expression and would appreciate it if you didn't use it around me.

- That implies there is a right way for boys and girls each to act, and I think it unnecessarily genders behaviors that are not gendered. Children climb trees. Humans make messes. People get mad. It's not just boys or men, and I'm not comfortable saying that it is.

- You're trying to excuse inappropriate behavior by claiming it's normal for certain children to act like that. What he did is not okay, and I'm concerned you are comfortable laughing off something so serious with a sexist cliche like "boys will be boys."

Sexuality

I identify as queer. I'm sexually and romantically attracted to masculine humans, generally cis men, trans men, butch lesbians, drag kings, and masculine nonbinary folk. For me, it's not about what's in their pants but what's in their eyes. I'm a total sucker for kind eyes. It's one of my favorite features of my partner, Sexy Beast.

As a member of the LGBTQIA+ community, I believe love is love. I think it's empowering for people to find the sexuality term that best fits how they feel, whether that's straight, queer, or any of the dozens of other possible sexualities. In this chapter I only included eight examples of the many different sexualities humans can identify with: asexual, bisexual, demisexual, gay, lesbian, pansexual, queer, and straight.

If you already are familiar with these eight, great! If you're not, today is the day to learn something new.

ASEXUAL

"You just haven't found the right person yet." "You haven't tried hard enough." "You just haven't found what kind of things turn you on."

- Asexual people exist. Just because you don't understand it doesn't mean it's not a real and valid way to be.

- I know you're trying to be supportive, but telling me that I don't know my own sexuality because it doesn't match yours is pretty offensive. A more helpful thing to say would be, "Asexuality is pretty unfamiliar to me. Will you share more about what you're experiencing?"

"Give me 10 minutes, and that won't be a problem anymore."

- That's a gross thing to say.

- Eww. Please don't say that to me or anyone else ever again.

"There's something wrong with you. Is it because you were hurt as a kid? Have you tried therapy?"

- Whoa. That's an offensive misconception about asexual people! Asexuality is both normal and healthy. There's nothing "wrong" with me.

- I get that asexuality is confusing for you because you're not asexual, but it's really dismissive of my experience when you say there's something "wrong" with me for not wanting to have sex like you do.

"Good luck finding someone who will put up with that." "I bet your spouse hates that." "Why would anyone want to be in a relationship with you?"

- I have value in a relationship beyond just sex. There's romantic, platonic, and domestic reasons to be with someone, and my partner(s) appreciate that.

- It's pretty disturbing that you'd reduce a complex emotional, intellectual, social, spiritual, and practical human connection down to just the sexual. There's a lot more to relationships than sex.

BISEXUAL

"How many women and men have you dated?"

- Nobody ever asks straight people how many people they've dated to figure out they're straight, so why are you asking me how many people I've dated to figure out I'm bisexual?

- Do you think there's a minimum number of partners someone needs to date to qualify for their sexuality?

"If you're bisexual, why have you dated so many men?"
"If you're bisexual, why did you marry a man?"

- Because I'm attracted to men. Bisexual isn't just "lesbian lite." I like both women *and* men.

- Dating men doesn't invalidate my bisexuality, and I don't appreciate you implying that it does.

"Do you like men or women more?"

- How could you ask me to pick one over the other when they're both so beautiful and unique?

- To me, men are attractive because they are solid yet tender, and women are attractive because they are soft yet fierce. I like them both for different reasons.

"Just asking . . . would you ever do a threesome?"

- With you? No, thank you. You're not my type. [They ask, "Why not?"] Because I'm not attracted to people who ask strangers for a threesome immediately after finding out they're bisexual. It's objectifying and not remotely sexy.

- I'm telling you that I love men for their kindness and strong hearts and I love women for their joy and bold words, and your first thought is to ask me if I'd sleep with you and your partner? Eww. No.

DEMISEXUAL

"I don't even know what that means! Why is everybody just making up newfangled sexualities all the time?"

- I get that lots of new terminology can be confusing. I'm not asking you to memorize the sexuality dictionary. I'm just asking that you respect me when I say I'm demisexual instead of accusing me of "making it up for attention."

- Why do you assume that anything you're unfamiliar with is made up? Isn't it possible there are sexualities you've just never come across before and don't know about?

"Does that mean you want to have sex with all your friends because you're emotionally close to them?"

- Are you genuinely asking because your intent is to learn, or are you trying to imply without stating outright that I am some type of promiscuous predator?

- Is your only experience with emotional closeness within your sexual relationships? Because it's common to have both friends and sexual partners.

"Oh, so you're a prude." "You're just picky." "You're afraid of sex."

- You're sounding pretty judgmental about me having a different sexuality than you. Why does this bother you so much?

- I love sex with partners I am emotionally close to. Why are you being so mean about it?

"Are you judging me for having casual sex?"

- Nope! You have your sexual expression and I have mine. I'm glad you're having fun!

- Just because I don't like carrots doesn't mean I would judge you for liking carrot cake. It's okay that we enjoy different things.

GAY

"Who's on top?"

- The way you're asking who's on top and who's on the bottom implies there's a hierarchy. There's not. We're equals.

- You seem to be really interested about how things happen in our bedroom. You know there's lots of information available online if you're curious, right?

"I could tell you're gay from your voice. You sound gay."

- If you mean that I'm not hiding my naturally animated inflections to try to sound tough, then yes, I do "sound gay."

- I encourage you to be careful about assuming someone's sexuality just based on their voice. A better bet is to let them tell you themselves.

"I don't care what you do in your bedroom, but you shouldn't be flaunting your sex life in public!"

- The only person talking about sex right now is you. Why are you determined to make our normal-married-couple-quick-kiss-good-bye into a sex thing?

- You obviously *do* care what we do in our bedroom because you're bringing it up.

"Just to play devil's advocate here, if a man and a man can be together, doesn't that mean [insert hurtful stereotype here]?"

- I don't debate devil's advocates. Anyone speaking on behalf of oppression in the interest of a false fairness is not initiating a conversation I'm willing to have.

- It might be "playing devil's advocate" to you, but it comes across as "your humanity is debatable" to me.

- Oppression doesn't require your advocacy. Maybe your intention wasn't to come across in a bigoted way, but it kind of sounds like you're "playing devil's advocate" so you can safely say bigoted things without taking ownership for those oppressive views.

- In my experience, a lot of people "play devil's advocate" so they can say hurtful things without taking any responsibility for the pain that they're causing.

LESBIAN

"Is this just a phase?"

- No. But even if it is, that's okay. The moon has phases too.
- I know you're curious, but asking questions like that is perpetuating hurtful stereotypes about women loving women. Being a lesbian is a valid sexuality. Definitely not a phase.

"Aren't all lesbians supposed to be butch? Like short hair and suits or something?"

- Lesbians are women who love women. Women look all different types of ways, including long hair and lipstick or short hair and sneakers.
- Nope. That's a myth. There are butches, studs, bois, femmes, lipstick or chapstick lesbians, and more. Women who love women come in lots of different types.

"Who wears the pants? Like which one of you is the man?"

- It's like you're asking who is the fork and who's the spoon when we're chopsticks.

- Everyone at our house wears pants. There are no men. That's what it means to be lesbians.

"Girl-on-girl! Hot!"

- I don't exist for your entertainment. Please leave me alone.

- It sounds like you don't know any lesbians outside of porn categories, and if you continue making inappropriate jokes like that, you probably never will.

PANSEXUAL

"How can someone be attracted to everyone?"

- My attraction to someone isn't limited by their gender. I like men and women (both cis and trans) as well nonbinary folk, agender individuals, and gender fluid people.

- If this is something you're really wanting to understand, the best option would be doing some learning online, because I can only give you one pansexual person's perspective.

"Isn't that just the same thing as bisexuality?"

- To me it's different from being bisexual, which I define as being attracted to two genders: women and men. Pansexual means attracted to all genders.

- There is crossover, and different people define bisexuality and pansexuality differently. Pansexual is the term that feels right to me.

"Why can't you just pick a side? Are you greedy?"

- There are no sides. There's a kaleidoscope of genders in the world and, yes, I'm greedy enough to be attracted to all of them!

- I don't have to prove the validity of my experience to you, so I am not going to. Let's talk about something else.

"So you'll sleep with anyone and everyone?"

- Pansexual doesn't mean promiscuous, but it does mean I'm attracted to a broad range of humans!

- You're attracted to women, but does that mean you'd sleep with any and all women?

QUEER

"Now you're just making stuff up for attention!"

- I get that humans will do all kinds of extreme things to get their needs met, but I really don't think pretending to be queer is one of them.

- I disagree that people are "just making stuff up for attention," but even if they are, that's okay with me. Humans need attention. That's really normal. If someone's in a position to make stuff up to get it, that means they're not getting enough support otherwise.

"But what about when . . ." [asking for intimate explicit sexual details]

- Are you asking all these questions about our sex life because you really want to learn? Because there's some good resources online I can refer you to that will explain this a lot better than I can.

- I'm pretty sure you're asking in good faith, so I'm going to say this in the kindest way possible: That's a really inappropriately personal question. Please google that on an incognito window if you really need to know.

"That's against the Bible!"

- If you're referring to Leviticus 18:22, the translation changed from "man shall not lie with young boys" to "man shall not lie with man" in the RSV translation of the Bible in 1946.

- Of the seven Biblical texts used to justify hate against queer people, the original translations are all about prostitution, cults, pederasty, and rape. Nothing about homosexuality. I can send you a great paper about it by Robert K. Gnuse if you're interested.

"Why would you choose that?"

- Did you choose to be straight? When?

- If you're trying to start a debate, it's not working. My sexuality is valid, whether you agree with it or not.

STRAIGHT

"You've had sex with how many people? Wow! You're a stud!"

- I appreciate that you're trying to celebrate me, but I don't think that's how that works. Studliness is based on skill level, not partner count.

- Why do we make a big deal about some people having a high sex partner count like it's a good thing, but for other people it's a bad thing? It's just a thing. It just is.

"You've had sex with how many people? Eww. You're used up."

- Sex is not a finite resource. You can't "use it up." It's unlimited and renewable.

- You asked what my sex partner count is and now you're being judgmental about it? Why did you ask like it's an open-ended question, but now you're acting like there's a right and wrong answer?

"You buy your girlfriend tampons when she has her period? What are you, gay?"

- I'm sad for you that you think demonstrating care to someone you love when they're in need is a sign of weakness. I hope you figure that out.

- I'm not okay with you using "gay" as a synonym for weak. My gay friends are some of the fiercest people I know.

"Don't you want a 1950s-style relationship? Where men are men and women are women?"

- I'd never want to yuck someone's yum, but 1950s role-play is just not our kink.

- Copying 70-year-old gender roles from before women could have bank accounts isn't my thing. But you do you!

Transgender, Nonbinary, & Gender-Creative

Trans, nonbinary, and gender-creative people have existed since ancient times in cultures around the world. Yes, the terminology keeps changing as humans continue to explore our understanding of gender identity, but people who are *more than* have always been here.

Thanks to the Internet, society's general familiarity with transness has expanded beyond maybe the one or few people who live locally to now an entire trans community seen, connected, and celebrated online. With this increased visibility, there has unfortunately also been a rise in vitriolic hate toward trans people.

It hurts my heart.

I love my trans, nonbinary, and gender-creative friends. I have several people I'm personally close with who are *more than,* and I wrote this chapter thinking of them.

While the statements here quoting what people say about trans, nonbinary, and gender-creative people are hateful, my "say the thing" responses are filled with love. Cherishing, honoring, protective, defensive, powerful, I'm-so-over-bigots-who-fear-what-they-don't-understand love! Let's dive in.

"Are you a boy or a girl?"

- I am an adult who is not going to answer invasive questions from strangers.

- I get that you're curious, but that is not any of your business.

- Is there some reason beyond general curiosity that you need to know?

"But what are you really?"

- I'm not sure if you are intentionally being offensive or you're acting out of unfortunate ignorance, but what you just said is transphobic, and I'm not going to continue this conversation.

- That is not an okay question to ask. A better option is, "Will you suggest your favorite online resource for learning about nonbinary people? I have some questions."

- I know that you are just curious and don't mean any harm, but that question is offensive. A better option if you really need to know for legal or medical reasons is, "Were you assigned male or female at birth?"

"What've you got 'down there'?"

- I don't talk about my genitals with anyone but my doctor. It's completely inappropriate that you asked me that.

- I think you're just being curious and not trying to be rude, but that is a terrible question. The better option is saying, "I have some misconceptions about trans people that I want to fix. May I ask you questions, or is it better if I look it up online?"

- Usually I'm happy to answer questions, but the way you're asking that comes across like I owe you intimate details about my life and body. I don't.

"So you're the third gender? *She, he,* and now *they?*"

- The most supportive choice you could make right now is to take responsibility for learning the basics of the trans experience instead of asking me to do your homework for you.

- It's not fair and it's not okay to put the burden on me to educate you about the basics of the trans experience. Please first google the questions that you're tempted to ask me.

- I get that this is brand-new to you, but this is something I've been answering questions about for [X number of] years. It would mean a lot to me if you would just google it instead of expecting me to do the work of educating you.

"What the heck does nonbinary mean? I'm so confused."

- Nonbinary is *more than* two genders. *Binary* means *two*, in this case man and woman. So nonbinary people are between, beyond, or bigger than the gender binary.

- Yes, terminology keeps evolving as we attempt to accurately capture in words the complexity of the human experience. It's okay to learn new words and definitions.

"Science says there are only two biological sexes."

- Are you defining "biological sexes" by chromosomes, hormone levels, external genitals, reproductive organs, or secondary sex characteristics? Because those are all different and don't necessarily divide into two distinct groups.

- If you're not willing to expand your understanding beyond high school biology, then we don't have anything to talk about on this subject.

"You're in the wrong bathroom."

- This is the bathroom I was assigned. Excuse me.

- This is the bathroom I was told to use. You're welcome to wait outside until I'm done; I'll only be a moment.

- I'm just here to pee and leave, just like you. Excuse me.

"Being trans is wrong."

- Trans people have always existed and will always exist. If that's "wrong," then I don't want to be right!

- I'm not going to debate you about the validity of my personal experience.

- It's understandable for you to be uneducated about the history of trans people. It's not okay for you to make bigoted statements about them. If you want to understand, there are plenty of good resources available online.

"You're just confused."

- It's okay for my gender identity to be an ever-evolving journey. That's not confusion; that's courage.

- It's not my job to educate you on my gender.

- The only thing I'm confused about is how my gender is any of your business?

"Trans women aren't real women!"

- Unless a trans woman is asking you to date her, why do you care?

- I'm really surprised that you're so bothered by this! I know you care a lot about personal freedom. What's more free than someone expressing themselves however they want in a way that doesn't hurt anybody? That's totally aligned with your values!

- You seem quite upset about this. Is this something you've personally experienced? Have you met a trans woman and felt attracted to her and then found out she's trans, which made you confront your own feelings about gender and sexuality, which was uncomfortable for you? Because you're talking like this is an issue you've had happen multiple times in your own life. Or are you just hating people you've never actually met?

"You're mentally ill."

- Living in a society that tells me I shouldn't exist because I'm gender creative has had an adverse effect on my mental health, yes.

- Am I trans because I have mental and emotional health issues? No, absolutely not. Do I have mental and emotional health issues because people keep attacking me for being openly trans? Yes, definitely.

"You're a danger to children." "You're a groomer." If they are saying this to you:

- No. Trans adults are living proof to trans children they can have a life where they can be themselves.

- No. You're using intentionally scary language to hide the fact that I'm existing peacefully, and you're attacking me right now in defense of some hypothetical children. Please leave me alone.

If you're a bystander when they are saying this to or about someone else:

- No. Being trans doesn't make someone a danger to children. Villainizing diversity is ignorant and bigoted.

- No. Your misuse of the term *groomer* is harmful to abuse survivors by diluting what happened to them as well as a total lie about trans people. It's not okay to say that.

"It seems like everybody is pretending to be trans these days."

- I think we're starting to see a more accurate representation of how many people are actually transgender. It's not increasing the number of trans people who exist, but it *is* increasing the number who are out about it.

- Considering the trans teen and adult mortality rate, I don't think anyone is "pretending" to be trans.

- People who really want to learn about this topic will do their own research instead of demanding answers to invasive questions in a public forum.

"Don't call me 'cis'! That's a slur! I'm just a regular woman!"

- When I use the word *cis*, it's a modifier to describe someone who identifies with their assigned birth gender. Since it sounds like that's you, that's why I used that term. It's okay if you personally don't use that word to describe yourself but that doesn't mean *cis* is a slur.

- It's transphobic to say "cis" is a slur.

- I can tell I'm not going to change your mind on this, so let's just move on.

- I get that you're afraid of what you don't understand, but I won't get stuck in an argument about it with you.

They refer to you as being "born in the wrong body."

- I'm in the right body; the doctor who assigned me male at birth got it wrong.

- I know some people use that language to describe themselves. I personally don't and would appreciate it if you didn't either. A better phrase is, "incorrectly assigned female at birth."

- My body is right. Society's definitions of gender are wrong. Please don't say that I am "born in the wrong body." Thanks!

My Favorite Go-To Boundary Phrases

If you don't find your topic in the alphabetical list, or if you still feel stumped by a question, you can always come here to the favorites list. These sample responses can be adapted to many different conversations and situations.

- I'm not available for [that], but what I can do is [this].

- May I share something with you that it seems you may not know?

- I appreciate your curiosity, but that is not a question I'm going to answer. Let's change the subject.

- That's not going to work for me. What else can we do?

- When you say [what they said], it comes across like [how it really sounds in direct language]. Is that what you meant?

- I know your intention is to be helpful, but that came across in a pretty hurtful way. What would be more helpful would be [suggestion].

- Are you trying to start a conversation about [topic]? Because a better option would be asking, [suggested language].

- I get that you're just curious and don't mean any harm, but that's a very intrusive question to ask a stranger, and it's not one I'm going to answer.

- I don't owe you any information. It is your responsibility to educate yourself on topics like this one.

- I know that you have good intentions, but you're asking me to do a lot of emotional labor to educate you on information that you could quickly find online.

- What I'm hearing you say is [repeat what they said in your own words]. Is that what you meant?

- May I ask you a clarifying question about what you're doing? It's okay to say no.

You're Doing Better Than You Know

We may not have had the opportunity to speak together in person, but if you've made it to the end of this book, I know a few key things about you:

You are putting in the time and effort to become better at boundary setting.

You are focused on practicing your kind and direct communication.

You're saying the thing.

That means you are doing better than you probably know.

We often underestimate how well we're doing, and I am confident you're most likely more accomplished than you realize. Be proud of yourself for choosing to do something different from what has been done in your family before. You're a leader, a pioneer, a guide.

When you practice saying the thing, you give other people permission to do the same. Then they in turn give more people that same permission by modeling clear and kind communication. It will continue to spread and grow, helping us all communicate effectively with one another. Each time you practice your boundaries, you're making the world a kinder place.

It's now the end of our one-on-one educational afternoon that I imagined back in the introduction. A day of fuzzy blankets, yummy snacks, and deep conversation. I wish I could've had you over to visit in person, but thankfully we got to connect through this book.

You're always welcome back! I hope you will continue to reference the topic sections you need boundary phrase support for whenever other people make curious, intrusive, or rude comments to you.

If you'd like to share with me which parts of this book resonated with you, please leave an online review, send me an email, or a comment on my TikTok, Instagram, or YouTube. I'd love to hear from you, and it will help other people find this book!

Say the thing,

Kami Orange
Boundary Coach
she/her

Suggested Further Reading

If you're looking for more information about the categories covered in *Say the Thing*, here are 12 suggested books and a brief description of why I recommend them.

Ask a Manager: How to Navigate Clueless Colleagues, Lunch-Stealing Bosses, and the Rest of Your Life at Work
by Alison Green

I've been a daily reader of Alison Green's blog *"Ask a Manager"* since 2015, and plus I've read every archived post since she began writing in 2007. I'm a big fan of her highly professional yet emotionally sensitive advice. If you need workplace support, I suggest both the book and blog!

Adult Children of Emotionally Immature Parents: How to Heal from Distant, Rejecting, or Self-Involved Parents
by Lindsay C. Gibson

Most of my boundary coaching clients were raised by emotionally immature parents or guardians. Being more mature than the person who raised you can make trying to say the thing feel like navigating a minefield. If that's you, you'll probably find clinical psychologist Lindsay C. Gibson's work to be transformative.

No Bad Parts: Healing Trauma and Restoring Wholeness with the Internal Family Systems Model
by Richard Schwartz

The idea that I have multiple aspects or "parts" of myself existing simultaneously (that often have competing needs and desires) has become the cornerstone of my self-compassion practice. Reading this book by Richard Schwartz is the equivalent of three years of trauma-focused therapy. Knowing my "parts" helped me feel whole.

What We Don't Talk About When We Talk About Fat
by Aubrey Gordon

As a fat person, this book gave me power and pride. There is something transformative about finding your community, and the work of Aubrey Gordon is that for me. From her podcast Maintenance Phase to her numerous articles to her books, I recommend her work to everyone; fat and thin alike.

Belly of the Beast:
The Politics of Anti-Fatness as Anti-Blackness
by Da'Shaun L. Harrison

Once you see it, you can't unsee it: the correlation between anti-fatness and anti-Blackness. This book is short in pages but deep in concept. Da'Shaun L. Harrison is a visionary abolitionist and has a perspective on the intersections of queerness, transness, fatness, and Blackness that forever changed how I think.

So You Want to Talk About Race
by Ijeoma Oluo

In this book, each chapter is formatted as a question about race and answered by the brilliant Ijeoma Oluo. It offered answers with the facts my brain required and the stories my heart craved. Especially as a white woman in America, this book is the anti-racism resource I return to again and again.

Read This to Get Smarter: About Race, Class, Gender, Disability, & More
by Blair Imani

I really appreciate the clear and concise nature of Blair Imani's writing, especially the chapter on class politics that goes over labor, wealth hoarding, socialism versus capitalism, etc. This book covers concepts I was already familiar with, but it helped me be more exact in how I speak about them.

Polysecure: Attachment, Trauma, and Consensual Non-Monogamy
by Jessica Fern

This is my favorite relationship book from both a monogamous and non-monogamous perspective. Jessica Fern gives a solid explanation of how trauma impacts our ability to form healthy attachments in any relationship. I recommend this book to everyone, but especially non-monogamous folks!

Speaking from the Heart: 18 Languages for Modern Love by **Anne Hodder-Shipp**
Knowing what "love" looks and feels like to me with my family, friends, partners, and/or myself has dramatically improved my life. This book explores love from a broader perspective than just five romantic love languages. Anne Hodder-Shipp prioritizes inclusivity in their writing which matters to me as a queer person.

Fair Play: A Game-Changing Solution for When You Have Too Much to Do (and More Life to Live)
by Eve Rodsky

I often give this book as a housewarming or wedding present because I'm happily using the Fair Play system in my own home! I adore the way Eve Rodsky applies her professional expertise in foundation management to household management. It's a relationship book masquerading as a "to-do list" guide.

Come As You Are: Revised and Updated: The Surprising New Science That Will Transform Your Sex Life
by Emily Nagoski

I've had substantially better sex since reading this book. It's a science-heavy read interspersed with engaging stories by Emily Nagoski. The information about anatomy, how stress affects our ability to experience pleasure, and arousal non-concordance is so groundbreaking. I know, it sounds really academic, but I promise it's worth reading!

The Seven Necessary Sins for Women and Girls
by Mona Eltahawy

This book made me gasp, weep, scream, belly-laugh, and then immediately read it all over again. The permission given by feminist giant Mona Eltahawy to fully choose what she calls the "seven necessary sins" of anger, attention, profanity, ambition, power, violence, and lust permanently changed me as a person.

Acknowledgments

Kelsey, it's not a baby, but I wish I could name this book after you.

A huge thank you to Linda Brown! You're my friend and my target audience. Love you!

I'm grateful to the Hay House team, especially Allison Janice for reaching out to ask if I wanted to publish a book and to Ashten Evans for being my editor.

Thank you to Alex Hogy, Anne-Lise Jasinski, Arabella B., Brandy Petersen, Brittany Galland, Dianne Nola, Donna Evans, Julie R., Lauren Gaboury, Mariah Cotter, Melanie Mulrooney, Michelle Drumm, Nicole, S.J. Nesbitt, Story Kiser, Susie Joy Torres, Tammy, Tara, and all my other clients, students, and followers for contributing. It's better because of you!

For coming in at the final hour and feeding me across the finish line, a huge thank you to Sexy Beast! I couldn't have done it without you.

About the Author

Kami Orange (she/her) is a boundary coach, author, and fat, queer, autistic, white, cis woman with over 17 years of experience helping people set boundaries, speak up in defense of others, and say the things that need to be said!

An international keynote speaker featured on BuzzFeed, Upworthy, CNN Health, morning television, and various podcasts, she's also on TikTok, Instagram, YouTube, and **kamiorange.com.**

We hope you enjoyed this Hay House book. If you'd like to receive our online catalog featuring additional information on Hay House books and products, or if you'd like to find out more about the Hay Foundation, please contact:

Hay House, Inc., P.O. Box 5100, Carlsbad, CA 92018-5100
(760) 431-7695 or (800) 654-5126
(760) 431-6948 (fax) or (800) 650-5115 (fax)
www.hayhouse.com® • www.hayfoundation.org

———

Published in Australia by: Hay House Australia Pty. Ltd.,
18/36 Ralph St., Alexandria NSW 2015
Phone: 612-9669-4299 • *Fax:* 612-9669-4144
www.hayhouse.com.au

Published in the United Kingdom by: Hay House UK, Ltd.,
The Sixth Floor, Watson House, 54 Baker Street, London W1U 7BU
Phone: +44 (0)20 3927 7290 • *Fax:* +44 (0)20 3927 7291
www.hayhouse.co.uk

Published in India by: Hay House Publishers India,
Muskaan Complex, Plot No. 3, B-2, Vasant Kunj, New Delhi 110 070
Phone: 91-11-4176-1620 • *Fax:* 91-11-4176-1630
www.hayhouse.co.in

———

Access New Knowledge.
Anytime. Anywhere.

Learn and evolve at your own pace
with the world's leading experts.

www.hayhouseU.com